G000021511

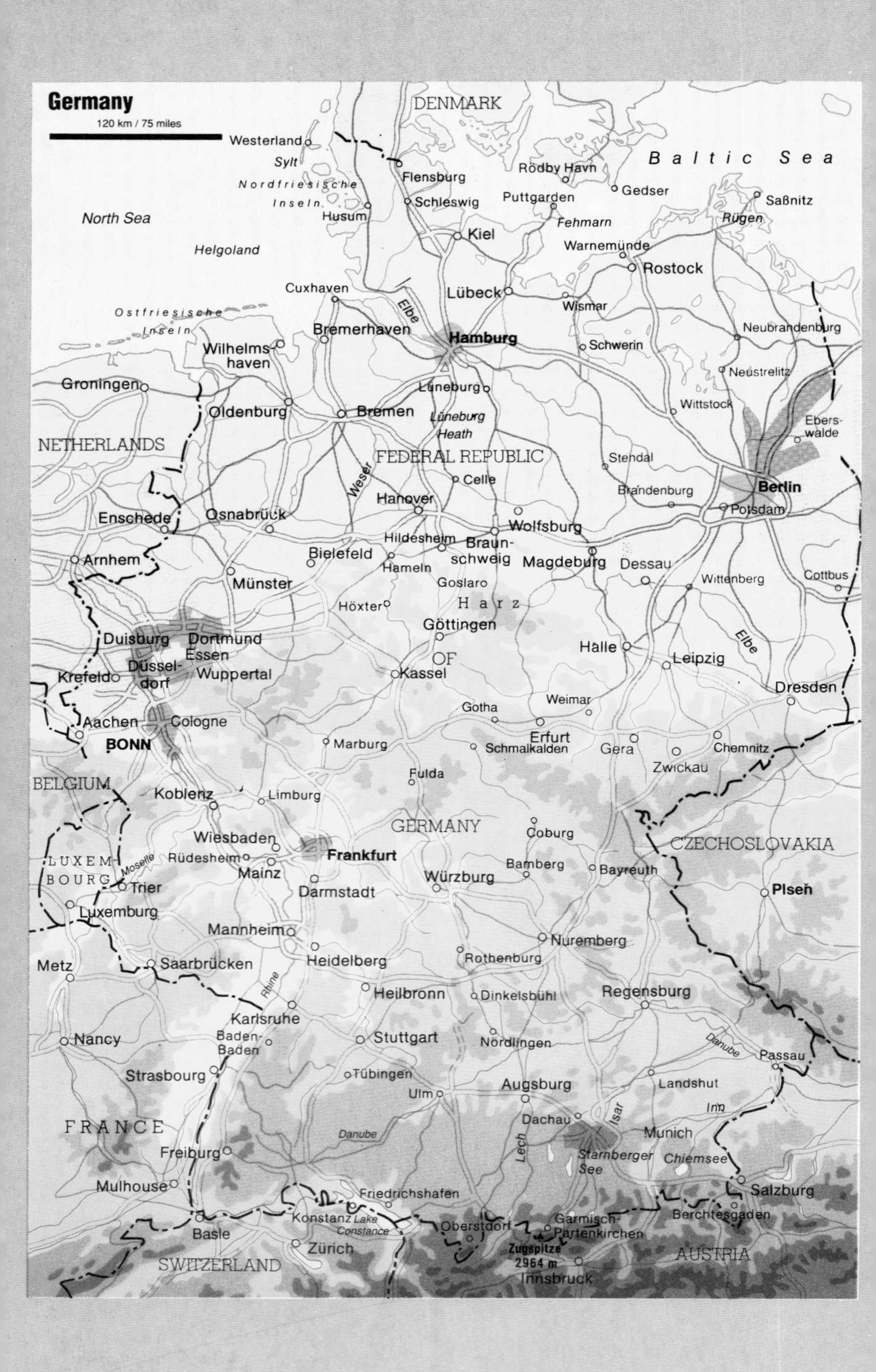
Germany
120 km / 75 miles
DENMARK
Baltic Sea
North Sea
Westerland
Sylt
Nordfriesische Inseln
Husum
Flensburg
Schleswig
Rödby Havn
Gedser
Puttgarden
Fehmarn
Saßnitz
Rügen
Kiel
Helgoland
Warnemünde
Rostock
Cuxhaven
Lübeck
Wismar
Elbe
Ostfriesische Inseln
Bremerhaven
Hamburg
Neubrandenburg
Wilhelmshaven
Schwerin
Neustrelitz
Groningen
Lüneburg
Oldenburg
Bremen
Lüneburg Heath
Wittstock
Eberswalde
NETHERLANDS
FEDERAL REPUBLIC
Stendal
Weser
Celle
Berlin
Brandenburg
Hanover
Potsdam
Enschede
Osnabrück
Wolfsburg
Hildesheim
Braunschweig
Arnhem
Bielefeld
Magdeburg
Dessau
Hameln
Münster
Goslaro
Wittenberg
Cottbus
Höxter
Harz
Göttingen
Duisburg
Dortmund
Essen
Halle
Elbe
OF
Leipzig
Krefeld
Düsseldorf
Wuppertal
Kassel
Dresden
Gotha
Weimar
Aachen
Cologne
BONN
Erfurt
Marburg
Schmalkalden
Gera
Chemnitz
Zwickau
Fulda
BELGIUM
Koblenz
Limburg
GERMANY
Coburg
Wiesbaden
CZECHOSLOVAKIA
LUXEMBOURG
Moselle
Rüdesheim
Frankfurt
Bamberg
Bayreuth
Mainz
Trier
Würzburg
Plseň
Darmstadt
Luxemburg
Mannheim
Nuremberg
Metz
Saarbrücken
Heidelberg
Rothenburg
Rhine
Heilbronn
Dinkelsbühl
Regensburg
Karlsruhe
Baden-Baden
Nancy
Stuttgart
Nördlingen
Danube
Passau
Strasbourg
Tübingen
Augsburg
Landshut
Ulm
Inn
Dachau
Isar
FRANCE
Danube
Lech
Munich
Freiburg
Starnberger See
Chiemsee
Mulhouse
Salzburg
Friedrichshafen
Berchtesgaden
Konstanz
Lake Constance
Oberstdorf
Garmisch-Partenkirchen
Basle
Zürich
Zugspitze
2964 m
AUSTRIA
SWITZERLAND
Innsbruck

Welcome to Berlin, capital of the newly united Germany and destined to become a bridge between east and west Europe. This guide will show you the city in all its moods, and Johanna Behrend will act as your friend, host and companion. Johanna was born in Berlin and there is hardly a corner of this intriguing city which she does not know: as a child she played in the Charlottenburger Schloßpark; she studied at the Freie Universität in Dahlem; in Kreuzberg she worked for the city's social services; as a journalist she has come to know aspects of Berlin which you will not find on any picture postcard.

Insight Pocket Guide: Berlin first presents a brief survey of the city's varied history and culture, provides assistance with orientation problems and, describes the beginning and end of the Berlin Wall. The *Day Itineraries* section contains suggestions for your first three days in Berlin covering all the most important sights. Day 1 takes you from the Brandenburg Gate via the Allee Unter den Linden to Alexanderplatz and the Nikolai Quarter. The evening is dedicated to that 'shimmering boulevard', Kurfürstendamm. Day 2 takes in the Kreuzberg 'scene', and Day 3 'respectable' Berlin – Dahlem, with its museums and Grunewald.

In the *Pick & Mix* section, Johanna presents many suggestions for additional things to see and do. These include essential items, such as a tour of Museumsinsel and a guide to the main shopping streets, as well as whole-day excursions into the surrounding Brandenburg countryside. The guide ends with a calendar listing all the major events in Berlin's year, further shopping, eating and nightlife suggestions and all the most important and up-to-date information essential to a pleasant stay.

Insight Pocket Guide: Berlin is designed for active and inquisitive travellers intent on getting the most out of their visit to the city on the Spree. This book provides the inspiration and information you need to discover the city in all its variety, and to experience its diversity and contradictions as well as its unquestionably interesting and attractive features.

Tach! Welcome!

Insight Pocket Guide

First Edition

Printed in Singapore by:
Höfer Press (Pte) Ltd, Singapore

INSIGHT POCKET GUIDES

BERLIN

Author **Johanna Behrend**
Publisher **Hans Höfer**
Design Concept **V Barl**
Designer **Willi Friedrich**
Photographer **Christine Engel**
Managing Editor **Andrew Eames**
Editor **Elizabeth Boleman-Herring**

Contents

Maps

Berlin has always had an overwhelming attraction uniquely its own, above and beyond that generated by any ties of patriotism, family and friendship. There is something in the Berlin air, a tingling, which keeps Berliners from dwelling on the past, compels us to seek change, and fosters the certainty, or the illusion, that the city is heading for an exciting and important future. My own extended stay in provincial West Germany only served to make me realise more acutely that seductive Berlin will eventually lure back anyone who has ever lived here. The city is like a smouldering coal. Supposedly burnt out, it only takes a breath of wind to rekindle its flames, sending out sparks that are capable of igniting a vast fire – as history has repeatedly shown us. Berlin was and is a breeding ground for innovation. Things happen here. Here the political and cultural spirit of the times is unfolding, and every individual has an opportunity to exert an influence. Berlin is no place for sitting back and taking it easy.

The decades of the city's division have in no way diminished its drive. Despite being an island engulfed by Communist East Germany – or perhaps *because* of this – the 'grand social experiment' has long been an integral part of everyday life. In East Berlin – immediately adjacent, yet incredibly distant – our *doppelgänger* went about creating a totally different world, rooted in another century. The friction between political-psychological opposites – East and West – generated a tension which kept the city, and often the entire world, in suspense. Not surprisingly, the newly unified city is characterised by contrasts: petty bourgeois mentality colliding with cosmopolitan urbanity; alternative lifestyles contrasting with established society; sylvan enclaves competing with sprawling satellite towns – and even a traditional hostility towards foreigners does not rule out cordial hospitality.

In Berlin everyone has a choice – although nobody *has* to make one. There is hardly a Berliner who can look back upon a life that

has not undergone fundamental change.

And that is exactly what makes life so exciting here. To strangers newly arrived in the city, this creative tension first manifests itself in the form of restlessness, hectic activity. Berliners are always busy; there is never enough time; always a new project in the offing. But, ironically, they also know how to postpone appointments and, sometimes, thay can make lots of time. When the sun comes out and Wannsee Beach beckons, or when an interesting chat in a pub goes on all night and Monday morning's scheduled meeting is forgotten, you will see the other, less driven side of Berlin.

Since the fall of the Berlin Wall, the city has become more crowded. The differences between the East and the West have begun to collide unbuffered. Now that Berlin has has re-established itself as an international metropolis, there are some isolationists who want to shut out the rest of the world. But real Berliners come from all four corners of the earth, and being a Berliner is not so much a matter of birthplace as it is a vigorous commitment to life, and life in this city. Every visitor who approaches Berlin with a spirit of acceptance and adventure, who visits not only the glorious avenues but also the 'grimy' nooks, will absorb some of this energy and perhaps become a Berliner – or at least leave enough of his or her heart behind in Berlin to make returning here a little like coming home.

Johanna Behrend

A Tale of Two Cities

Berlin's 750th birthday in 1987 was honoured with great pomp by both the Senate (on the west side of the wall) and the Magistrate (on the east). It had to be a double celebration, of course. After all, Berlin would not be Berlin if it did not overdo everything, but the boisterous twin cities of the post-war era are a far cry from their small and modest 13th-century forebears.

In those days, the swampy area along the River Spree was not exactly inviting terrain for settlers, with annual floods constantly threatening home and possessions. One spot, however, was somewhat drier than the rest. At this point two important German trade routes met and crossed, one going north/south and the other east/west. A pair of clever traders set up shop here, founding not one but two towns: Cölln and Berlin. Thus began the history of the great metropolis: as twin towns surrounded by swamps.

In the year 1411, a feudal lord from Nuremberg purchased both towns from the emperor for 400,000 guilders. Frederick IV – who six years later would be named Elector Frederick I by Emperor Sigismund – established the Hohenzollern

Frederick William I in Friedrichstadt

ture

dynasty, which was to last for over 500 years.

In 1643 a man ascended the throne who was to lay the foundation for Berlin's cultural and military supremacy: Frederick William, later to be named Grand Elector. He fortified the city – which had been devastated by the Thirty Years War – and established new outer districts. Under his aegis the Huguenots found asylum when religious persecution drove them from their home in France. This was a boon to Berlin for it was through their influence that the clever, but otherwise rather uncouth, Berliners gained access to culture and learned a more refined way of living.

Frederick the Great with greyhound

Frederick II, the son of the Grand Elector, was an ardent admirer of the splendid court of Versailles. Not only did he attempt to imitate Louis XIV's *savoir vivre*, but in 1701 he also crowned himself king – not exactly in compliance with monarchic tradition – which is why he only titled himself Frederick I *in* Prussia. Under his authority Berlin and Cölln, along with the three outlying districts, were united in 1710 to form one city: Berlin. The next king, Frederick William I, however, put an end to the baroque lifestyle introduced by his father. Frugal to the point of meanness, he had a soft spot for his personal regiment of 'Lange Kerls' – named after its unusually tall soldiers – and went down in history as the 'soldier king'.

Berliners did not breathe easily until Frederick II attained the throne. Well-educated and culturally refined, the soldier king's son established Berlin's reputation as the 'Athens on the Spree'. Frederick the Great, as he is known to posterity, laid out the Forum Fridericianum on Unter den Linden – including the first building in the complex, the Opernhaus – and he went on to build Schloß Sanssouci in Potsdam, surely the most beautiful castle complex in the region of the Brandenburg Marches.

The period which followed saw the growth of the outer districts of the city along with the appearance of numerous factories, leading to the first conflicts between social classes. During the early 19th century, demand grew for far more than image and status. Banners

Detail of the monument of the Great Elector

were raised calling for freedom of the press and freedom of speech, while the burgeoning proletariat called out for bread and employment. The conflict came to a head during the March Revolution of 1848, but was quelled by military force a few months later.

Around the middle of the 19th century, Berlin developed into an industrial city. Tenements were thrown up overnight to house the necessary labour force. War then abruptly altered not only Berlin's status but also the situation throughout Europe. Prussia's victorious campaign against France in 1870–1 gained the Prussian king, William I, the vacant German emperor's throne.

Great and Dashed Expectations

The effect on Berlin was a boom of unforeseen proportions. During these years of rapid German industrial expansion, property speculation reached fever pitch, allowing many Berliners to make quick fortunes – and, often, to lose them just as quickly. The mass housing built for the poorer tiers of the urban population began to establish Berlin's reputation for having the largest concentration of tenement houses in the world; at the same time the rural road called Kurfürstendamm was being developed into a splendid boulevard. Berlin became a magnet for artists and scientists, but also attracted increasing numbers of unemployed.

In 1914, at the beginning of World War I, Berlin's upswing collapsed. The longer the war lasted, the more massive and radical the protests became. When the war ended in defeat in 1918, soldiers in Kiel mutinied and hundreds of thousands of workers throughout the nation took part in protest marches. The emperor abdicated on 9 November 1918, whereupon the Republic was proclaimed twice: by the Communist Karl Liebknecht at the Stadtschloß and by the Social Democrat Philipp Schneidemann in the Reichstag, the German parliament.

For the first time in its history, Germany was now a republic, but at the other end of the political spectrum, the nationalistic German volunteer corps, the Freikorps, did not warm to the idea of republic at all. Bloody street fighting was the order of the day – and in Munich the National Socialist movement began to gather momentum, with the aim of first conquering Berlin; then the entire world. In the wake of the world economic crisis, the 1933 Reichstag election produced results with serious consequences: Hitler had himself appointed Reichskanzler, and shortly afterwards the Reichstag was deprived of its power – marking the beginning of the Nazi dictatorship. Jews were banished from public life and the Nazis' political opponents were persecuted or killed. These events eventually sparked off World War II and the holocaust – making the Prussian metropolis, Berlin, synonymous with terror and death.

In 1945, the Nazi nightmare was brought to an end – but by then Berlin was in ruins. The former capital, the Reichshauptstadt, was divided up into zones by the four victorious powers, laying the groundwork for the subsequent division of the city. Berlin's development into two very different halves did not actually begin until 1961, when the Communist GDR (German Democratic Rupublic) regime erected the Berlin Wall – allegedly to defend its own borders. It took constant transfusions of West German capital to keep the artificially walled-in city alive and well and to maintain its appearance as a 'Showcase of the Western World' in the middle of a Communist state. East Berlin, on the other hand, was outfitted with grand buildings – befitting its role as the 'Capital of the GDR'.

It seemed Berlin would remain a divided city indefinitely. As an 'island', West Berlin became a magnet for dropouts and for the left-

Goebbels' Berlin speech inciting war

Parade celebrating the 35th anniversary of the GDR

orientated protest movement, while East Berlin became the centre of power for a stubborn, geriatric regime. Until 1989, that is, when a wave of dramatic change swept through the GDR and all of Eastern Europe – leading to the fall of the wall on 9 November 1989. Once again, Berlin became the scene of events determining the fate of Central Europe. Since 3 October 1990, and the reunification of the German states, Berlin has been steadily renewing itself as a single city. Only time will tell what role Berlin will play in the new rapprochement between East and West.

Artwork along the wall

The Wall That Was

Was für London der Tower, ist für Berlin die Mauer. This flippant slogan comparing the Berlin Wall with the Tower of London is now obsolete. The wall, once Berlin's main tourist attraction, has vanished – demolished, its debris swept away by the winds of change. There is nothing left of this structure, as murderous as it was 'picturesque', with all its painting and graffiti – unless you visit a museum or are one of the monied few who managed to buy a segment at the Cannes auction during the summer of 1990.

The erection of the wall which was to surround West Berlin for nearly 28 years was every bit as surprising as its fall. During the night of 12 August 1961, Berliners were confronted with a *fait accompli*: soldiers and members of the workers' militia leapt out of their military lorries, unrolled barbed wire along the sector boundary and immediately began laying the first bricks. The stunned Berliners on both sides were to suffer the consequences of a conflict which had been smouldering for some time. For years the special status of West Berlin had been a bone of contention between

Erecting the Berlin Wall

the USA and the USSR. Khruschev, the Soviet leader at that time, demanded the withdrawal of Allied troops from the 'autonomous political entity of West Berlin', stating among other reasons, that the GDR felt threatened by this enclave of capitalist activity. West Berlin was the only escape route for thousands of people fed up with the crumbling and repressive socialist state. At the beginning of August 1961, Walter Ulbricht, the leader of the SED, the ruling East German Communist party, was called to Moscow. A few days later, on 13 August, West Berlin was walled in.

Securing the border at the Brandenburger Tor

During the months and years following, numerous people attempted to flee from the East to the West: leaping from windows overlooking the wall, digging tunnels, giving their last pennies to helpers who smuggled them across the border under harrowing circumstances. Some simply, and hopelessly, climbed. For many, the attempt ended in death, and after each incident the SED had the structure even more elaborately fortified. Eventually, the wall included an additional 'death strip' – 50m (165ft) wide, at night lit by floodlights, and guarded by sentries and dogs. The few openings were secured by a series of sophisticated devices. Over the years, West Berliners came to terms with the wall, although no-one ever accepted it. Artists, graffiti-sprayers and communicative visitors turned the wall into the longest work of art in the world – and the most frequently photographed object in the city. The fallow land in front of it developed into an almost pastoral parkland.

In the eastern part of Berlin the entire area along the wall was a prohibited zone – off-limits to everyone. Many a curious citizen interested only in taking a closer look at the 'monster' was arrested for 'attempted illegal border-crossing'. The wall was only open to visitors from the West – though the visiting procedure involved obtaining a visa and observing extremely bureaucratic border controls. The only East Berliners allowed to pass through the checkpoints to the West were top officials, senior citizens or *personae non gratae* – dissidents who were not allowed to return.

The fall of this symbol of a divided Berlin came just as unexpectedly as its appearance. The mass exodus of East German citizens across the Austrian/Hungarian border and their storming of the West German embassies in Warsaw, Prague and Budapest finally prompted those who had stayed at home to demand reforms. As before the building of the wall, the GDR was losing its citizens. Beginning in Leipzig, demonstrations quickly spread to other East German cities. Erich Honecker, the last SED leader, was forced to resign along with several of his comrades. On 4 November 1989, half a million people gathered on an East Berlin square, the Alexanderplatz – voicing their protest in no uncertain terms. Five days later at a press conference held on 9 November 1989, the SED government announced, almost in passing, that travel restrictions for GDR citizens had been lifted. That very night, people from East Berlin flooded into the western part of the city. The images of that night in Berlin were broadcast live around the world. Hundreds of thousands celebrated throughout the city and the frenzy of enthusiasm lasted for weeks.

The ultimate razing of the wall happened much more quickly than its construction. Thousands of *mauerspechte*, or 'wall-peckers', as they were called, chipped small chunks out of the concrete surface – either to keep as souvenirs or to sell. Demolition firms and People's Army troops lifted entire slabs out of their foundations for sheer commercial purposes, at least as far as the most brightly-painted sections were concerned. The unpainted slabs located on the edge of town, on the other hand, were crushed – producing gravel needed for reconstructing the roads which had been cut between the East and the West.

The actual wall has now disappeared, but it has left visible scars in the form of fallow land. The people of Berlin also bear the scars of the wall – in their alienation from one another. Shaped by totally different political-cultural experiences, their values and expectations now clash, sometimes leading to physical conflict. The fallow land will soon have disappeared – developers are already fighting over the choicest plots. Needless to say, it will take the people of the two Berlins some time to mend the rift that divides them and to overcome their estrangement.

East German soldiers erecting barbed wire fences

Getting Your Bearings

Berlin is a huge city that encompasses four rivers, about 50 lakes, numerous islands and plenty of forest; four airports (one restricted to military use), five long-distance train stations, a ring-road for automobile traffic and a circle line for the suburban railway; districts with their own town centres and 3.5 million garrulous inhabitants – each of whom, if asked, will provide a different set of directions for how to get to any one place. Given all this, it might be helpful to have some basic orientation of your own.

Arriving by plane, you will land either at Tegel to the north, at Schönefeld to the south-east or – less frequently – at Tempelhof, right in the middle of the city, though generally this airport is used by only a few domestic airlines. Berlin Tegel airport's distinguishing feature is its compactness. From the landing gate, brought to the door of the plane, visitors go straight into the baggage hall; from there it is just a few steps to the taxi rank or bus stop. From both Tegel and Schönefeld you can take a bus into the 'Western' city to the area of the Bahnhof Zoo and Kurfürsten-damm. Entering Berlin by taxi is easier, of course. From Tegel it is a quick drive

Alexanderplatz station

via the urban motorway to just about any part of central Berlin. Schönefeld is out of town, so the taxi ride takes a little longer.

When arriving by train, get off at either the Bahnhof Zoo or the Friedrichstraße station, depending on where your hotel is. From 'Zoo' you can reach most hotels around the Kurfürstendamm in a matter of minutes. Most of the hotels in the east of the city are concentrated around Alexanderplatz and Unter den Linden and if you are based here, the Friedrichstraße station is closer. Either way, you will arrive near the city centre: at either the 'Kudamm' (short for Kurfürstendamm), or Unter den Linden.

A word of warning to anyone arriving by car: although the map shows thoroughfares designed for driving straight from one end of town to the other with no major detours, here, just as on the urban motorways, you can easily get stuck in one of the city's infamous traffic jams. Moreover, it may take less time to drive from Berlin to Hamburg than to find a parking place near the Kurfürstendamm – a situation that can only worsen in the future.

Show girls in the Haus Vaterland

A City That Never Sleeps

Berliners like to have a good time, so there is constantly plenty on the city's cultural agenda. There are more cultural institutions here than in any other German city; there always have been, and now many of them exist in duplicate – one in the west and one in the east. The four museum complexes alone – the island of Museumsinsel in Berlin-Mitte, Schloß Charlottenburg, the Kulturforum and the museums in Dahlem – house some of the most significant works of art in the world; and there are countless smaller museums scattered throughout the length and breadth of the city.

Berlin now has more theatres than it can fund, as well as two opera houses competing for international acclaim. During the mid-1980s Götz Friedrich took over the directorship of the Theater des Westens, where producer and choreographer Helmut Baumann's intelligently designed Kurt Weill revue and cosmopolitan *Cageful of*

Idiots were rapturously received. The city's historic theatre, the Schauspielhaus, has been converted into a concert hall, but the music temple par excellence remains, without a doubt, the world famous Philharmonie – even without its former director. Founded in 1882, the 'Berliner Philharmonisches Orchester' played itself into the international limelight principally under the directorship of Herbert von Karajan. At the end of von Karajan's era it was rated as being one of the best orchestras in the world. You can enjoy show entertainment at the Friedrichspalast or, a bit more off-beat but no less elegant, at the Varieté im Quartier.

Berlin would not be Berlin, however, without the less traditional forms of amusement. The small 'underground' theatres provide the impetus for innovative theatrical art. The Tempodrom circus tent is a major venue for concerts from the alternative cultural scene, whereas the Quasimodo is reserved for jazz and rock. If you still want more, there are nearly a hundred cinemas screening a broad range of films, and countless discothèques, nightclubs and satirical shows to choose from. After all, Berlin is open around the clock – all you need is the stamina to take it all in.

Discarded symbolism

Historical Outline

1237 First recorded reference to Cölln-Berlin.
1319 End of Askanian dynasty's rule. Berlin is claimed by various houses, but is ruled by no-one.
1417 Elector Frederick I establishes Hohenzollern rule.
1539 Elector Joachim II aligns himself with Luther.
1640–88 Regency of the Great Elector Frederick William. Edict of Potsdam brings Huguenots to Berlin: Berlin's cultural ascendancy and Baroque influence begin.
1701 Elector Frederick II crowns himself king in Prussia. Development of outlying districts and founding of Academy of Sciences.
1710 Cölln and Berlin combined together with three outlying districts into united municipality.
1713–40 Frederick William I turns Berlin into a garrison town; builds a wall to prevent the escape of potential soldiers.
1740–86 Frederick II (the Great) comes to power; Berlin becomes a cultural centre. Schloß Sanssouci and Forum Fridericianum built.
1791 Construction of the Brandenburger Tor.
1810 University founded on the initiative of Wilhelm Humboldt.
1815 First buildings designed by Prussian architect Karl Schinke.
1848 Bourgeoisie question king's claim to absolute power; growing proletariat demand better living conditions. Revolution in March quelled by the army.
1871 King William I is crowned German Emperor at Versailles. Numerous firms and societies are founded in the 'Gründerzeit' boom known as founders' era.
1888 Kaiser William II ascends the emperor's throne.
1914 The Kaiser declares war on France and Russia, triggering World War I.
1918 After the Armistice, soldiers' rebellion and a popular uprising, the last Hohenzollern ruler steps down.
1920 Reform draws eight cities and around 60 communities together, creating Greater Berlin.
1933 30 January, Hitler seizes power; 27 February, the Reichstag fire. By 10 May books are being burnt on Opernplatz.
1936 Berlin hosts the Olympics; Hitler demonstrates his power.
1939 Germany attacks Poland starting World War II.
1945 After 12 days of fighting, Berlin is defeated and in ruins. The Red Army occupies the city.
1948 Berlin Blockade: Soviet troops cut off roads and rail lines, forcing the Allies to provision Berlin's population by airlift.
1949 East Berlin becomes capital of the GDR.
1950 West Berlin is given a new constitution. Ernst Reuter elected its first mayor.
1961 Building of the Berlin Wall.
1968 Events in West Berlin trigger the revolution by German student.
1981 The squatters' movement makes Berlin once more a focal point of social change.
1987 West and East Berlin celebrate their 750th anniversary, separately.
1989 On 9 November, after 28 years, the Berlin Wall is breached.
1990 First election of a joint municipal parliament for East and West Berlin since 1946.
1991 Berlin named capital of reunified Germany.

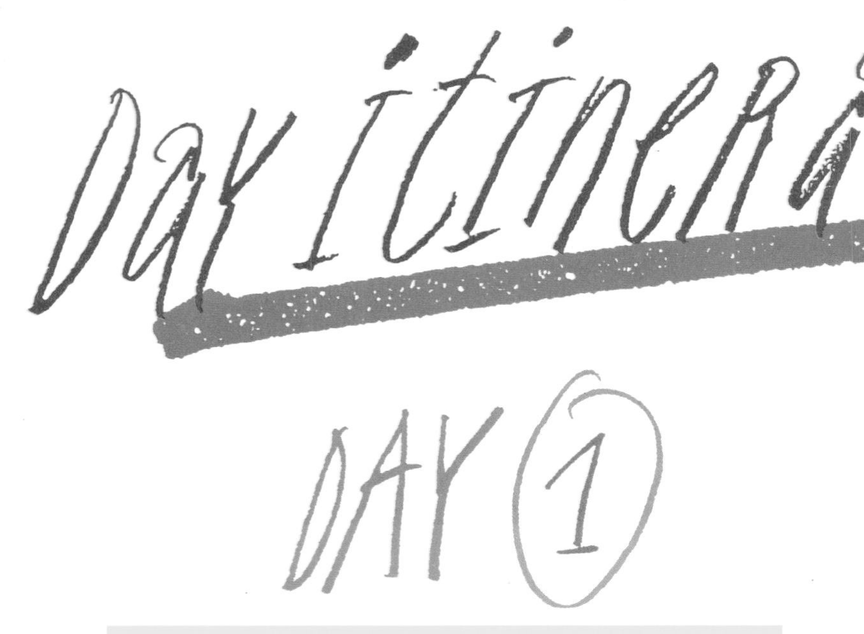

Prussian Splendour

A stroll along the Prussian boulevard, Unter den Linden, from the Brandenburger Tor to Alexanderplatz and the Fernsehturm; through the historic centre, the Nikolai Quarter and on, to spend the evening on the lively 'Kudamm'.

–To Starting Point: S-Bahn station: Unter den Linden; or taxi, ask for 'Brandenburger Tor'–

Coming up from the S-Bahn (Underground) or getting out of a taxi, the overwhelming sight of the **Brandenburger Tor** (Brandenburg Gate) is immediately obvious. The symbol of national consciousness ever since it went up in 1791, it has been the symbol of German unity since the division of Berlin. Crowning the gate, the **Quadriga** represents the Goddess of Victory pulled by a team of four horses. Contrary to certain rumours, her direction of movement has always been eastward. Following Victory's proud gaze, march between the columns and through the gate. Following in the footsteps of triumphant monarchs and determined revolutionaries alike, proceed along the once magnificent boulevard, **Unter den Linden** (Under the Limes), straight into the heart of Berlin.

At first it takes a bit of imagination to picture this boulevard's former splendour. A great deal was destroyed here during the war. The leaders of the SED (the now-disbanded ruling communist 'Socialist Unified Party') were very slow to take an interest in Prussian traditions. But on mild June evenings, when the air is perfumed with the delicately sweet fragrance of linden trees, it is possible to put up with even the unadorned and functional buildings that line the street all the way to the Friedrichstraße intersection –

where history reappears in all its glory. Although built during the 1980s, even the **Grand Hotel** (corner of Friedrichstraße), with its revivalist design, is a feast for the eyes. Within the Grand Hotel, sensual pleasure of a different kind awaits us in the **Silhouette** restaurant – featuring some of the finest cuisine in town.

Now take in the rear view of the **equestrian statue** of **Frederick the Great** on the traffic island. Originally, 'Old Fritz', as he was affectionately called, had a clear view of his castle from here. Unfortunately, during the 1950s, overzealous 'historical Stalinists' tore the Hohenzollern palace down – replacing it with the **Palast der Republik**. Today the former seat of the East German Volkskammer, or 'People's Assembly', with its gleaming copper exterior, is closed due to asbestos contamination. This may explain the grumpy look on Frederick's face. He might find more reason to smile if he were to look to his left, catching a glimpse of old **Humboldt University** with its aura of dignity and tradition; or, for that matter, towards the square on his right, **Bebelplatz**, where – on what was then Opernplatz – he and his friend, the architect Georg Wenzeslaus, built their Forum Fridericianum, fulfilling a spiritual and cultural manifesto. The state opera house, the **Deutsche Staatsoper**, was the first building to go up. Opposite, the

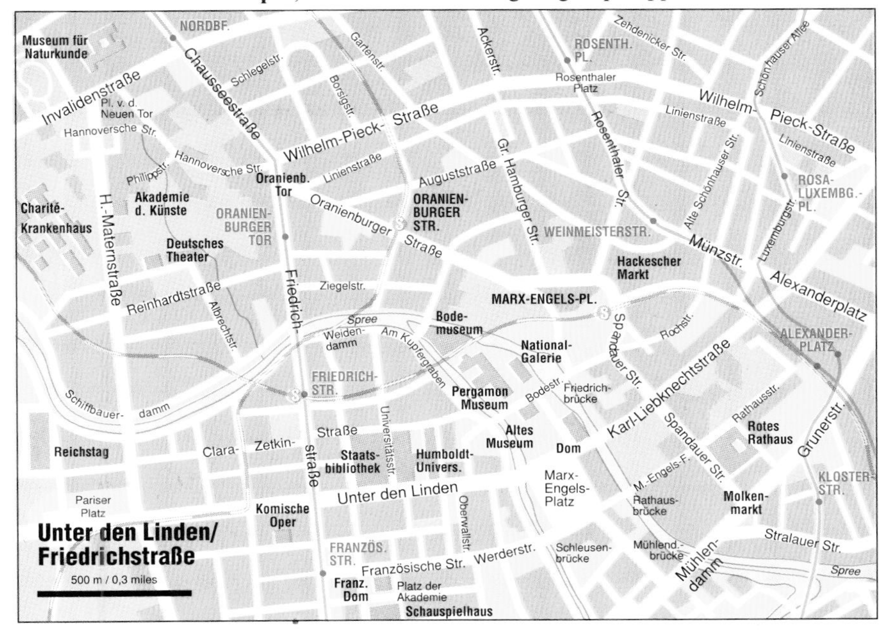

Statue of Frederick the Great, in front of the Humboldt University

Royal Library or **Königliche Bibliothek** – nicknamed the 'Chest of Drawers' after its curved form – was not added until later. Frederick also had the domed **St Hedwig's Cathedral** in the background erected in honour of the Silesian Catholics. A bit further along the 'Linden' the former princesses' palace, **Prinzessinnen-Palais**, today houses the **Operncafé**, an establishment combining a café, restaurant and discothèque. What better place for a coffee break? From here there is a wonderful view of the **Neue Wache** (New Guardhouse), the first building completed under Prussia's neoclassical architect, Karl Friedrich Schinkel. Under the GDR regime it was made a memorial to the victims of fascism and militarism. The ritual changing of the guard – complete with goose-stepping Prussian soldiers – is now, however, a thing of the past.

To the right of the Neue Wache is the former armory – and one of the most beautiful Baroque buildings in Berlin: the **Zeughaus** containing the **Museum für Deutsche Geschichte**. It is assumed that there will be a few changes in the museum's inventory – until recently, exhibits were geared towards presenting history from a socialist perspective. Now history, among many other things, is being adapted to new times and ideologies.

Across the bridge, **Marx-Engels Brücke**, is Spree Island, where Berlin's twin town of Cölln was founded during the 13th century. Ignore, for now, this museum island, since we will return later, on a tour focusing exclusively on it. Instead, direct your attention to the cathedral in the foreground of the Museumsinsel: the **Dom**. Scorned at the end of the last century as the epitome of Wilhelminian bad taste, with all its convolutions and heavy ornamentation, it seems downright charming today – in contrast to the sober **Palast der Republik**. Except, that is, on those occasions when the Dom is lit up at night – by green and purple spotlights: Kaiser Wilhelm (William II) would surely have loved it.

Leaving Spree Island via the other 'socialist' bridge, **Liebknecht-Brücke**, cross the **Marx-Engels-Forum**, pausing for what may be the last opportunity to look Karl Marx and Friedrich Engels in the eye – for the future of the two statues is uncertain. Some anonymous clown marked the monument's pedestal with the graffiti, *Wir sind unschuldig* ('We are innocent'), but those in charge of Berlin's civic politics do not seem all that convinced.

Next there is the windy expanse of that famous square, the **Alexanderplatz**. Not a sign remains of the bustling, cramped hub of business which thrived here during the 1920s. Surrounded by gigantic blocks of architecture, a human being feels tiny and lost. The **Weltzeituhr**, or 'world clock', a popular meeting point on the square, tells how late it is in Moscow, among other places. Perhaps Honecker, the former GDR leader, should have paid heed to it: having overlooked the signs of the times, he is now punished by history. The **Brunnen der Völkerfreundschaft** (Fountain of Friendship Among Nations) is always crowded with weary sightseers sitting around the perimeter and resting their feet. A visit to the the television tower, the **Fernsehturm,** with the futuristic structures around its base is a definite must. The 'ball' at the top offers the visitor a spectacular panoramic view of Berlin. In fact, in the revolving tower restaurant it is possible to just sit and watch the entire city slide by below. At the foot of this inspiring structure the

Alexanderplatz: a peaceful haven

small medieval church of **Marienkirche** seems almost to cower.

The **Rotes Rathaus**, or 'Red City Hall', derives its name not from its political bent but from the red bricks used as building material. In 1991 it became the seat of the All-Berlin Senate. In the vaults of the Ratskeller, by the way, you can get a good solid meal if you like Berlin's home-style cooking. The tiny access streets to the right of the Rathaus lead into the **Nikolai Quarter**, the 'cradle' of Berlin. The entire quarter is the prefab product of 'Real Socialist' concrete slab construction methods. Despite this, the replica of a medieval settlement is quite impressive. How tiny Berlin once was! The church right in the middle of the quarter, the **Nikolaikirche**, is the oldest building in Berlin. Even though they are imitations, the numerous 'old' shops and Old Berlin pubs radiate the charm of their builders' Prussian heritage.

The **Platz der Akademie**, which until the founding of the GDR used to be called Gendarmenmarkt (Gendarmes' Market), is the most beautiful square in Berlin. It features the theatre, or **Schauspielhaus**, Schinkel's masterpiece of neoclassical architecture, and the **Deutsche** and the **Französische Dom** with an excellent restaurant on its upper floors. These buildings provide a vivid impression of what Berlin, the 'Athens on the Spree', once looked like.

A stop at the **Dom Hotel** provides a welcome rest. After all, the nightlife along the **Kurfürstendamm**, or 'Kudamm' for short, is next on the itinerary. Of course you should come back here during the day when the shops are open; and there is an itinerary in the *Pick & Mix* section for all those interested. But night-time is when the boulevard really comes to life. All of Berlin – not just tourists – crowds the sidewalks day and night. The restaurants, cafés, pubs, street stands offering knick-knacks, and all the glitzy, flashing neon signs demonstrate what a major metropolis is all about. Here, even strolling at 3am, you will find yourself surrounded by people watching the street performers and pavement artists. The ruins of the old **Gedächtniskirche,** together with the new concrete church

Market in Alexanderplatz

A quiet corner in the Nikolai Quarter

next door, are the focal point of all this activity. And do not miss the **Europa-Center**. Founded in 1965, the centre houses some 100 stores, restaurants, bars and cafés; a cinema with five screens, a 'Multivision Show' offering a crash course in Berlin's history; a nightclub; a casino; a cabaret, and a revue theatre; Berlin's largest sauna and a 106-m (353-ft) tall platform with telescopes.

If you are hungry, make a detour to Meinekestraße 27, a few steps off the Kudamm, for an *eisbein* (pork knuckle with sauerkraut), a *schlachteplatte* (ham and sausage from freshly slaughtered pigs), *königsberger klopse* (meatballs) or, if you prefer, a *biersuppe* (beer soup), the latter concoction is also available as a beverage. The food is plentiful, so dig in – and then call it a (well-spent) day!

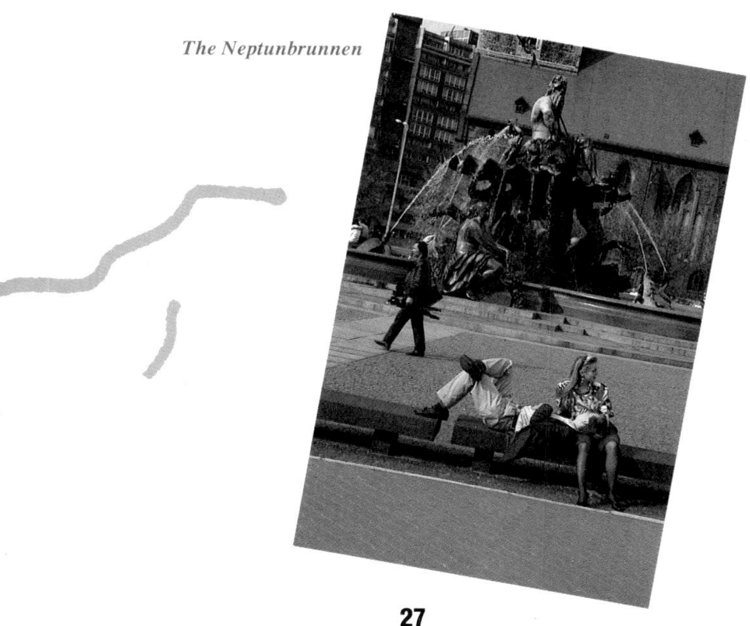

The Neptunbrunnen

The Kreuzberg Scene

A stroll through Kreuzberg with its motley multicultural scene, deep into the heart of SO (south-east) 36.

—To Starting Point: U-Bahn to Südstern station; or taxi, ask for 'Südstern'—

People refer to Kreuzberg as one entity, but there are actually two Kreuzbergs. First there is the – shall we say – up-and-coming western portion, Kreuzberg 61; and then there is Kreuzberg 36, known as **SO 36**. 'SO' stands for the old postal delivery zone 'South-east', which included Kreuzberg – an area whose dirty-faced charm attracts slummers from far and near, and where riots and squatters have been making the headlines for years.

Cautiously make your way into the heart of Kreuzberg, to **Südstern**. The 'star' in the square's German name refers to the seven streets that converge here. There is plenty going on, and with a café, pub or restaurant on every corner, this is one of the most popular centres of the underground scene. How about starting off with a snack at the **Rampenlicht** at the corner of Körtestraße? While you have coffee or a light lunch, you can gain a first impression of the artistic activity in this neighbourhood since the Rampenlicht also serves as a gallery for young Kreuzberg artists. Also on Körtestraße, you will find the first of many off-beat fashion boutiques and junk shops to explore. To reach the most beautiful spot in Kreuzberg, however, continue from the end of Körtestraße via Grimmstraße to the bank of the Landwehrkanal, the **Paul-Lincke-Ufer**. The canal is lined with old, restored town houses with pergola-covered front gardens – and again, lots of pubs and restaurants, bustling with a motley

Scrounging for food

crowd of colourful people, especially in summer. Not exactly elegant, the **Café am Ufer** nevertheless serves a 'Millionaire's Breakfast' (Dm160 for two) up until 4pm (for late risers!) – including salmon, caviar, champagne and everything else you might expect (or hope for) for breakfast. If you think such a thing out of place in Kreuzberg, then you have another thought coming – young couples in particular order this humble repast more often than you would imagine. You will also find one of the most elegant restaurants in Berlin located on the Paul-Lincke-Ufer (at No 44): the **Exil** (Tuesday–Sunday 7pm–3am) – one of the city's foremost gourmet temples and one which has popularized no-frills style in conjunction with excellent cuisine.

On Tuesday and Friday, the riverbank opposite is the scene of the so-called **Türkenmarkt**. Just plunge into the merry, noisy hustle and bustle of this weekly market with its rich array of oriental goods and allow yourself to be transported to a world of Turkish bazaars. Moving on, along Kottbußer Damm to Skalitzer Straße, we come to **Lausitzer Platz**. This square is more or less the entrance to the formerly outré section of Kreuzberg, regularly the scene of First of May street battles with the police in the 1980s. No need to be anxious here now though: the days of the street-fighters are over. Whole streets have now been redeveloped, with former squatters going straight and legalising their tenant status with properly signed leases.

Today, people here are having to cope with an entirely different predicament. The fall of the wall has meant the end of their niche-like existence on the city fringe. Suddenly, Kreuzberg has become part of a dynamic downtown business area; this transition has not only had a drastic affect on shop rents but has also threatened the inhabitants' sense of belonging within their own neighbourhood. Many a small shopkeeper or alternative craftsperson has already been forced to pack up and leave.

Critical buyers at the Türkenmarkt

U-Bahn station Schlesisches Tor

There is still a reminder of the neighbourhood's erstwhile 'counter culture' preserved in the former Bethanien Hospital on **Mariannenplatz**. The building in the middle of the square has been transformed into the **Kunstamt Kreuzberg** (Kreuzberg Art Bureau) – establishing a home for Turkish culture, exhibitions, meeting places and a library. **Georg-von-Rauch House**, the former Bethanien nurses' home, was the very first building in Berlin to be occupied by squatters. Since 1972 it has been run successfully by young people involved in self-administration. During the summer the green area is full of German and Turkish residents grilling meat, drinking, making music and celebrating. A theatre tent attracts visitors from all over town – causing business in the surrounding pubs to pick up abruptly once the show is over.

Setting course for the former town gate, Schlesisches Tor, proceed along **Wrangelstraße** – a typical Kreuzberg residential street of unadorned tenement houses with plenty of courtyards. Although most of the buildings have been thoroughly renovated, the cramped living conditions which prevailed here can still be sensed in the way the various structures are wedged and sandwiched together – immediately reminding some visitors of the proletarian street scenes in Zille's atmospheric turn-of-the-

century *Miljöh* ('milieu') paintings.

Turn left at **Skalitzer Straße**, a dead-end during the days of the Berlin Wall, with the elevated train, Line No 1, dismally clattering past on its way to the terminal at Schlesisches Tor. Also named the 'Orient Express', after the many Turks living here, the train's claim to international fame was the Grips Theatre's musical, *Linie 1*. Now, the cul-de-sac is no more; within the next few years the elevated train will be connected with its counterpart in the eastern part of the city, and Skalitzer Straße is in the process of becoming a more reputable shopping street. Another pedestrian-only zone in the shadow of the wall has found its days were numbered.

Before heading home, I suggest a stop at **Schlesisches Tor**, which should be as edifying as it is fortifying. The **Bagdad**, a Turkish restaurant with a misleading name, is a small oasis of oriental *savoir vivre*. Its intimate garden, rich Anatolian food, and authentic atmosphere will make you forget you are in the heart of Berlin. Sheltered from the outside world, this garden restaurant presents a display of oriental splendour which verges on kitsch. The fountain stocked with goldfish, arbours strung with coloured lights and the musician's drawn-out tones captivate not only the Turkish guests, but also many young German families who come here after weekend outings. At weekends, the treat of a belly-dancer in glittering, diaphanous costume swirling between the tables, sometimes causes even the waiters to forget their duties.

Boats on the Landwehrkanal

Dahlem: the Museum and Villa District

A tour of the Dahlem museums, a look at the former village structure of Berlin, and a stroll to the Jagdschloß Grunewald.

–To Starting Point: U-Bahn or taxi, ask for 'Dahlem-Dorf'–

Some of the most beautiful art treasures in the world are on display in Berlin. After all, collecting is one of the Berliner's great passions. And, of course, everything has to be just a bit bigger, better and more beautiful here than anywhere else. The visitor is begged to overlook this slight display of arrogance – it is, after all, quite justified, at least as far as the museum landscape is concerned. This book contains sections on all four of the museum centres: the Kulturforum, the Museumsinsel (Museum Island), Schloß Charlottenburg and Dahlem. Start off here with a visit to the complex in Dahlem, complementing this megadose of art with a relaxing outing to one of the most beautiful lakes in Berlin, the Grunewaldsee.

Begin, however, at the Museum of Ethnology, the **Museum für Völkerkunde** (daily except Monday 9am–5pm), on **Takustraße**. You will see first a selection of artefacts from the South Seas housed on the ground floor. With its eerie array of shrunken heads, the skull holder from New Guinea was hardly designed for use as a comfy headrest. But are the miniature noggins the real thing? The

In the Villa District

In the Gemäldegalerie

attendant answers with a cryptic smile. Turning away with a shudder, move on to the **Boat Hall**, which features sea-going vessels found in the South Seas: from dugout canoes to sailboats. Judging by the dreamy-eyed expressions on many visitors' faces, their thoughts are far away – in one of these exotic boats, riding the gentle waves of Polynesia, approaching a palm-lined beach...

A detour through the Pre-Colombian department – also located on the ground floor – is a definite must. The **Gold Room** is one of my favourite places in the museum. The gleam of the golden Mayan cult objects beats any display at Cartier. The ceremonial knife with a golden handle bearing the merciless visage of a deity is particularly striking. The knife was reputedly used for cutting out the hearts of human sacrificial victims.

From the Museum of Ethnology, move straight into the Painting Gallery, the **Gemäldegalerie** (closed Monday), and head upstairs to Room 236 to pay a brief visit to the most famous man in Berlin: *The Man with the Golden Helmet.* Although recently revealed to be the work of a pupil, instead of the Master himself, it is still hanging in the **Rembrandt Room**. Nor has its 'exposure' in any way damaged the attraction of this portrait of a weary warrior. The expression of fatigue, as well as the awareness of the wretchedness of death on the battlefield etched into this man's face, are of particular relevance today – when 'conventional' warfare is apparently becoming a 'viable option' again.

The painting is usually surrounded by a cluster of people. The other rooms are quieter. In Room 236, for example, around the corner to the left, you will find Caravaggio's *Amor as Victor*: a boy with a mischievous smile and arrows in hand, glides from a rumpled bed, beside which is thrown a suit of armour – as if Love's defeated opponent could not discard it quickly enough to slip into the bed of his beloved. A very pleasurable alternative indeed to waging war, and much more productive, as well.

Returning to the ground floor, stop at Room 109A to round out this sensual tour with a look at Correggio's *Leda with the Swan* before heading for the main entrance to re-emerge onto Arnimallee.

The entrance to the **Museums of Indian, Islamic and Eastern Asian Art** on **Lansstraße**. The entire array of oriental splendour – precious carpets, figurines of dancing gods, delicate paintings – will transport you to an exotic world. By now you may have begun to feel hungry, so why not nip down to the **Alter Krug Dahlem** at Königin-Luise-Straße 52. Classified as an official monument, this rustic tavern, a farmhouse dating back to 1785, conveys an impression of Dahlem's pastoral past. The menu features good plain cooking, wholefood dishes and 40 different wines. Thus fortified, cross the street to the **Domäne Dahlem**, a former electoral farming

On the shores of the Grunewaldsee

operation dating from the 17th century. The old manor house, practically a royal country seat, houses a museum documenting the work and leisure on a Brandenburg Marches estate. Stables for cows and horses and a barn exhibiting old farming implements are grouped around the manor house. The seasonal festivities are merry events and include the *Schlachtefest*, a feast featuring freshly slaughtered and prepared pork, and *Erntedank* (Thanksgiving). On such occasions, Berliners enjoy slicing juicy hunks of meat off whole pigs roasting over an open fire, washing this down with generous quantities of beer.

Königin-Luise-Straße leads directly into Grunewald. Head straight down the forest road to arrive at one of the most idyllic spots on the lake, the Grunewaldsee: the **Jagdschloß Grunewald** is a hunting lodge dating from the 16th century. Its old walls house a museum (10am–6pm, closed Monday). The displays include hunting accessories as well as paintings by Rubens and Lucas Cranach. At such a distance from their castles and their lawfully wedded wives,

Morning riders

the electoral princes apparently had other things on their minds – judging by the erotic paintings on the walls. At night the halls are said to be haunted by the ghost of an electoral mistress who had fallen out of favour. Who else would want to visit a museum at night, anyway?

For the evening, I recommend a special culinary delight. At **Matterhornstraße 101** in **Nikolassee** you will find the best restaurant in town: **Frühsammers Restaurant An der Rehwiese** ('Frühsammer's Restaurant by the Deer Meadow'). Reservations are definitely recommended (Tel: 803 2720). You can get there via the S-Bahn station 'Nikolassee', but taking a taxi is a better alternative. The restaurant is quite a way out of town, but it is well worth the trek. The combination of *haute cuisine*, the finest wines and stylish ambience provides a fitting end to a day so full of cultural discovery.

The Jagdschloß Grunewald

1. On Museum Island

A visit to the unique museum complex in the centre of Berlin.

–To Starting Point: S-Bahn station Marx-Engels-Platz; or taxi, ask for 'Lustgarten'–

Historically speaking the Nikolai Quarter is the centre of Berlin, whereas the centre of amusement is indisputably the Kurfürstendamm. But the actual hub of Berlin is the spot from which the city's reputation as a cultural metropolis grew: the island of **Museumsinsel**. The buildings themselves are an enchanting sight and the treasures on display inside the museum complex are among the most significant works of art in the world.

The most impressive approach to the complex is via the **Lustgarten**. Rising up in the background, the **Altes Museum** (Wednesday–Sunday 9am–6pm) was built on what was once the royal kitchen garden (where the first asparagus and potatoes were grown in Prussia) and later the parade ground. With its 18 Doric columns and flanked by bronze statues of the *Fighting Amazon* and the *Lion Wrestler*, it looks like the entrance to a shrine. Karl Friedrich Schinkel actually modelled the building on a Greek temple in 1830. Instead of sublime Greek artefacts, however, the interior has a surprise in store: GDR art, the entire body of official state painting. 'What is to become of the products of socialist state culture?' is a popular topic of current discussion. But rather than dwelling on this – there are well paid people in 'higher places' already racking their

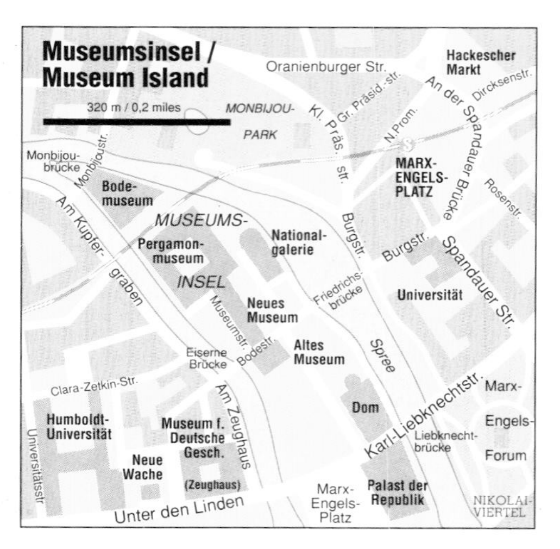

brains over it – let us move on to the gallery of copperplate engravings, including a collection of drawings, on the ground floor. The gallery also includes an exhibit detailing Schinkel's artistic legacy. The drawings clearly reveal what the Prussian architect would have built if only he had been allowed.

Since the war the **Neues Museum**, immediately behind the old, has remained a tragic ruin. The reconstruction has been dragging on for years. With the current state of Berlin's finances it is anyone's guess when it will be finished. Also designed to resemble a Greek temple, the dainty **National-Galerie** (Wednesday–Sunday 9am–6pm) features, in addition to Expressionism, Bauhaus and New Functionalism, an extensive collection of works by sculptor Johann Gottfried Schadow. His most popular work, by the way, is perched prominently on top of the Brandenburg Gate: the Goddess of Victory with her team of four horses.

The most famous building on the island, however, is the **Pergamon Museum** (daily 9am–6pm) housing one of the largest collections of art of the ancient world. The superlative is no exaggeration. The famous *Pergamon Altar,* consecrated to the Greek goddess Athena

Monuments of ancient cultures in the Pergamon Museum

The Monbijou bridge

over 2,000 years ago in Asia Minor, was reconstructed using the original fragments inside a huge room designed specially for this purpose. Another relic of ancient civilisations is the monumental Roman *Market Gate of Milet*. In some places you can still detect the markings for the traders' stands. Indeed, some of the dark stains on the old stone surface may derive from pre-Christian tomatoes, carelessly squashed millennia ago…

To me the most impressive display is upstairs: the *Procession Boulevard of Babylon* leading to the *Ishtar Gate*. The magnificent blue of the glazed tiles – although for the most part reproductions – convey an impression of the former splendour of the land between the Tigris and the Euphrates. The **Islamisches Museum** and the **Ostasiatische Sammlung** (Eastern Asian Collection) have been installed on the second floor. For a particularly remarkable experience, however, do not miss the Folklore Museum, the **Museum für Volkskunde**, on the mezzanine. This small exhibition of clothing has everything from peasant costumes to early 1980s GDR-produced textiles (terrible stuff styled for a 'model Real Socialist' look). The section on the 1970s raises a smile with its figure clad in Indian shirt, jeans and a parka with a Palestinian 'fedayeen cloth' around its neck. (Who would ever have thought that the 'uniform' of my youth would end up in a museum collection, let alone the Pergamon Museum?)

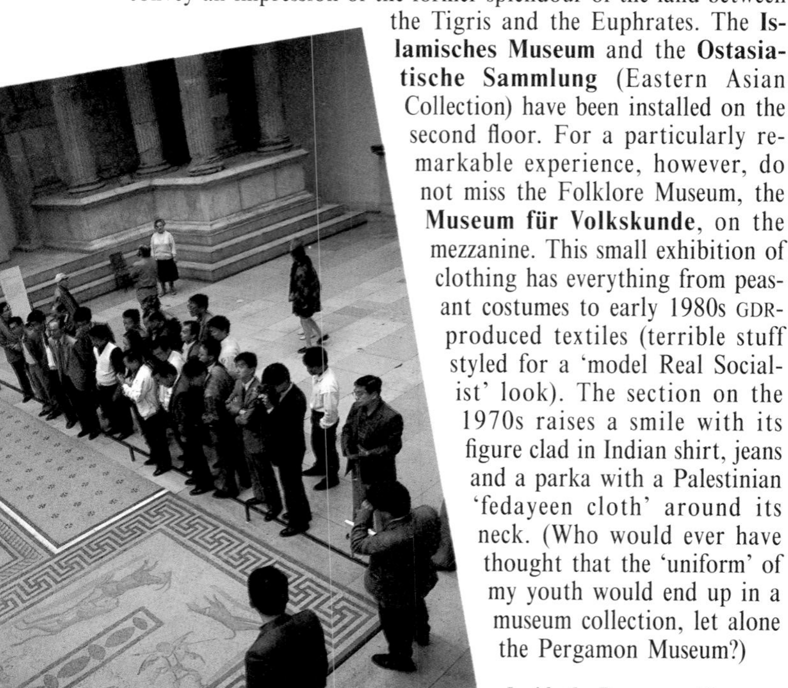

Inside the Pergamon Museum

The **Bode-Museum** (Wednesday–Sunday 9am–6pm), the latest building, dating from the turn of the century, covers three subjects. I definitely recommend the **Ägyptisches Museum** (Egyptian Museum). It offers a splendid presentation of the ancient cult of the dead – with mummies, coffins, burial chambers and cult objects providing an eerie picture of Death on the Nile. It even includes a sarcophagus for the mummy of a cat, the sacred animal of the goddess Bastet. The papyrus collection calls for another superlative: it is the largest in the world, containing approximately 30,000 texts.

Moving upstairs, the mood switches from the spiritual to the material, as brief tribute is paid to filthy lucre. The **Münzkabinett** (Numismatic Museum) displays approximately 500,000 items. The coins, medals, seals and notes give an idea of what has run through the hands of mankind over the course of centuries. There is a hint of malice in the eagerness with which many await the addition of the 'Aluchips' – as the scrapped lightweight coinage of the now-defunct GDR was dismissively called.

Also upstairs, the **Gemäldegalerie** (Painting Gallery) contains mainly German, Italian and Dutch masters from the 15th to the 18th century and you should tour the collection now if you resisted it on Day 3. In addition to some 25 Rembrandts, there are magnificent examples of virtually every movement in Western art before 1800. From the Italian School are works by Giotto, Botticelli, Raphael and Titian; the German Gothic and Renaissance are represented by Dürer, Cranach and Holbein; and the Dutch include Breughel, Vermeer, Hals and Rubens.

However I head straight for the Rembrandts, the Master's *Moses Smashing the Tablets*, a painting which I cannot help viewing with a certain sense of envy when I think of what I myself would like to do to certain holy cows. But before succumbing to unholy thoughts, let us take another look at the sculpture collection on the ground floor of the Bodemuseum, at a few of the beautiful medieval Madonnas for example, before leaving Museum Island – edified and inspired by art – via the Kupfergraben (Copper Moat). One of the numerous street cafés there will provide some much needed and no doubt well deserved refreshment.

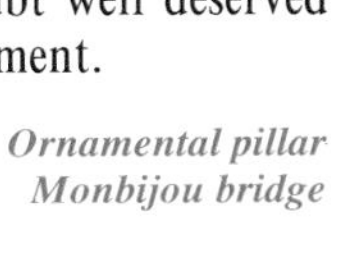

Ornamental pillar Monbijou bridge

2. In the Footsteps of Brecht

A walk along Friedrichstraße, past the Berliner Ensemble; a detour to the cemetery, Dorotheenstädtischer Friedhof; a visit to the Brecht House and on to the Museum of Natural History.

–To Starting Point: S-Bahn station Friedrichstraße; or taxi, ask for 'Schiffbauerdamm'–

At the famous train station **Bahnhof Friedrichstraße** we turn north, making our way to the Spree River. Looking to your left from the **Weidendammbrücke** bridge you will see the Berliner Ensemble theatre building – even easier to recognise at night when the name appears in green neon letters on the roof. It was here, in the **Theater am Schiffbauerdamm**, that Bertolt Brecht spent the post-war years perfecting his epic theatre. Over the years, however, the manner of presentation has begun to seem a bit fuddy-duddy. Brecht fans, though, will be interested to know that they are still showing the original stagings of the *Threepenny Opera* – which premiered here in 1928 – and also *Mother Courage*. Even under the communists, the **Ganymed Restaurant** (Monday 5pm–1am, Tuesday–Sunday 11am–

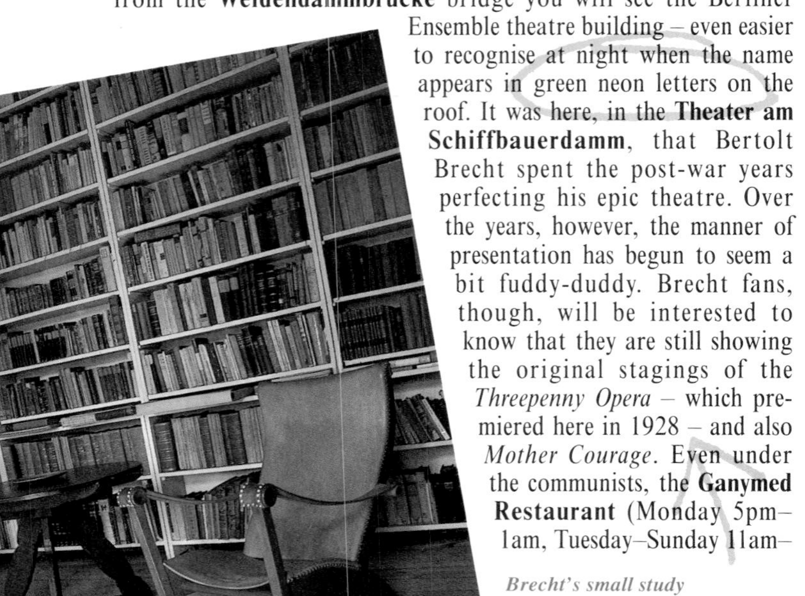

Brecht's small study

1am) next door was one of the most renowned 'wine restaurants' in Berlin. Actors still often drop in for a light snack after the show.

Crossing the bridge, continue along the part of Friedrichstraße which, in the 1920s, was famous for its predominantly shady establishments. It has kept its slightly sleazy charm despite the waning notoriety of its places of amusement. The **Friedrichstadtpalast** (you cannot miss it on the right-hand side, with its oriental façade), for example, one would have to call quite respectable despite its restrained 'Erotic Show'.

A look around the former town gate, **Oranienburger Tor**, where the tram screeches around the corner, gives an impression of the old (and the new) poverty of this area. Oranienburger Straße – on the right – leads into the Scheunenviertel ('Barn Quarter'), the most run-down area in all Berlin. The huge ruin a short way down the street managed to withstand decades of demolition efforts on the part of the renewal-crazed SED (Communist Party) regime. In 1989,

The typewriter with which Brecht wrote his plays

just before the 'Wende', the change in government, it was occupied by artists and instilled with new, vibrant life under the name **Kulturzentrum Tacheles**. This entire area is the centre of Berlin's vanished Jewish quarter, the extinguished world of the city's 160,000 Jews. Today, only a few hundred of the Jewish community remain in 'East' Berlin. Their former synagogue in Oranienburger Straße (which was set on fire during Kristallnacht in 1938 and further damaged by bombing in World War II) remained a 'ruin of remembrance' until restoration was begun in 1985.

Now, however, it is time to pick up Brecht's trail again. At Oranienburger Tor, Friedrichstraße turns into Chausseestraße – where the playwright once lived. Before dealing with the living

Culture and decay

Brecht, however, let us pay a brief visit to his grave. The **Dorotheenstädtischer Friedhof**, on the left side of **Chausseestraße**, is certainly one of the most beautiful cemeteries in Berlin. Just to the left, hugging the cemetery wall, we find the graves of Brecht and his wife, Helene Weigel. Their final resting place is quite inconspicuous when compared with the impressive gravestones and splendid burial sites of the other celebrities interred here: Prussia's neoclassical architect, Karl Friedrich Schinkel, the philosopher Georg Friedrich Hegel and the writer Anna Seghers. You are sure to recognise other famous names as you stroll among the graves including that of Johann Gottlieb Fichte, the 18th century philosopher of the nationalistic Romantic school.

Directly behind the cemetery, at Chausseestraße 125, we come upon the first traces of Brecht's life in the form of his former residence. Brecht's and Weigel's living and working chambers were left in their original state and turned into the **Brecht Museum** (Tuesday–Friday 10–noon, Thursday 5–7pm, Saturday 9.30–noon, 12.30–2pm). Here you can imagine Brecht sitting in his armchair at the window of his study, gazing pensively at his future resting place or, perhaps, composing a new poem. The cellar of the house commemorates the poetic couple in a different fashion: the **Brechtkeller** serves dishes cooked according to Helene Weigel's recipes. Erich Honecker used to come here frequently. For those guests who have no taste for culinary art, there is also a choice of Viennese specialities. The walls

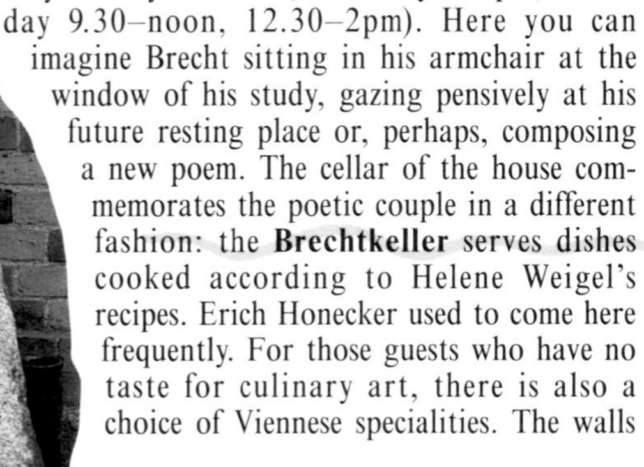

The grave of the playwright

Dorotheenstädtischer cemetery

are covered with pictures of Brecht, along with models of his stage sets. He would probably have approved of this healthy mixture of food for thought and stomach.

Before turning your attention to these pleasures, I recommend one more visit: to one of the oldest inhabitants of planet Earth – or at least what is left of it. To the right, on **Invalidenstraße**, you will find the Museum of Natural History, the **Naturkundemuseum** (Tuesday–Sunday 9.30am–5pm) which houses the zoological, mineral and paleontological collections of Humboldt University. Most importantly, however it also contains the largest dinosaur skeleton in the world. At 12m (40ft) in height and 23m (75ft) in length, the *Brachiosaurus brancai* makes you glad, as a diminutive human being, that these dainty creatures are extinct. The giant bones may, however, also bring out your Stone Age instincts and send you off in search of smaller, meatier game. If so, you can either make your way back to the Brechtkeller or take a taxi to the **Ermeler Haus** at Märkisches Ufer 10 (daily, 11am–12pm), a Baroque town house with a gourmet restaurant offering very stylish dining.

3. Schloß Charlottenburg

A visit to the castle with a walk around the Schloßgarten.

–To Starting Point: Buses 9, 54, 74, U-Bahn station Sophie-Charlotte-Platz; or taxi, ask for 'Schloß Charlottenburg'–

Once upon a time there was a beautiful princess who longed for nothing more than a small summer castle in a rural setting. And so it came to pass, in 1695, that her spouse, Frederick III, had his architect, Johann Arnold Nering, build a stately pleasure seat, naming it 'Lietzenburg' after the nearby village of Lietzow. In the year 1701, the elector – an ardent admirer of Versailles – crowned himself king, henceforth calling himself Frederick I, King of Prussia, and thus making Sophie Charlotte a queen. In 1705, however, the merry lady died, prompting the king to rename her favourite castle 'Charlottenburg'.

Arriving by bus, taxi or Underground, and before climbing the short distance to **Schloßstraße**, you will see this superb specimen of Prussian Baroque stretching out for 505m (1,656ft) along the bank of the Spandauer Damm, concealing an expansive park to its rear – one of the most beautiful in Berlin. Though all but destroyed in 1943, the actual castle was faithfully reconstructed after the war, a task which took decades. Today it serves as a museum (Tuesday–Sunday 9am–5pm). You can trace the steps of Queen Sophie Charlotte – even though the place has changed a bit since her day.

From the frontage first make your way to the western wing on the left, passing through the **Oval Room** and the **Oak Gallery**, where occasional chamber concerts are held. The last room of the suite is the **Porzellankabinett** (Porcelain Gallery), with its splendid display of porcelain from Japan and China. The finest, tiniest tea cups, richly ornamented vases, artfully painted plates and delicate

Schloß Charlottenburg

Dorotheenstädtischer cemetery

are covered with pictures of Brecht, along with models of his stage sets. He would probably have approved of this healthy mixture of food for thought and stomach.

Before turning your attention to these pleasures, I recommend one more visit: to one of the oldest inhabitants of planet Earth – or at least what is left of it. To the right, on **Invalidenstraße**, you will find the Museum of Natural History, the **Naturkundemuseum** (Tuesday–Sunday 9.30am–5pm) which houses the zoological, mineral and paleontological collections of Humboldt University. Most importantly, however it also contains the largest dinosaur skeleton in the world. At 12m (40ft) in height and 23m (75ft) in length, the *Brachiosaurus brancai* makes you glad, as a diminutive human being, that these dainty creatures are extinct. The giant bones may, however, also bring out your Stone Age instincts and send you off in search of smaller, meatier game. If so, you can either make your way back to the Brechtkeller or take a taxi to the **Ermeler Haus** at Märkisches Ufer 10 (daily, 11am–12pm), a Baroque town house with a gourmet restaurant offering very stylish dining.

3. Schloß Charlottenburg

A visit to the castle with a walk around the Schloßgarten.

–To Starting Point: Buses 9, 54, 74, U-Bahn station Sophie-Charlotte-Platz; or taxi, ask for 'Schloß Charlottenburg'–

Once upon a time there was a beautiful princess who longed for nothing more than a small summer castle in a rural setting. And so it came to pass, in 1695, that her spouse, Frederick III, had his architect, Johann Arnold Nering, build a stately pleasure seat, naming it 'Lietzenburg' after the nearby village of Lietzow. In the year 1701, the elector – an ardent admirer of Versailles – crowned himself king, henceforth calling himself Frederick I, King of Prussia, and thus making Sophie Charlotte a queen. In 1705, however, the merry lady died, prompting the king to rename her favourite castle 'Charlottenburg'.

Arriving by bus, taxi or Underground, and before climbing the short distance to **Schloßstraße**, you will see this superb specimen of Prussian Baroque stretching out for 505m (1,656ft) along the bank of the Spandauer Damm, concealing an expansive park to its rear – one of the most beautiful in Berlin. Though all but destroyed in 1943, the actual castle was faithfully reconstructed after the war, a task which took decades. Today it serves as a museum (Tuesday–Sunday 9am–5pm). You can trace the steps of Queen Sophie Charlotte – even though the place has changed a bit since her day.

From the frontage first make your way to the western wing on the left, passing through the **Oval Room** and the **Oak Gallery**, where occasional chamber concerts are held. The last room of the suite is the **Porzellankabinett** (Porcelain Gallery), with its splendid display of porcelain from Japan and China. The finest, tiniest tea cups, richly ornamented vases, artfully painted plates and delicate

Schloß Charlottenburg

A little rest

figurines are arranged along all the walls. Decorating mirrored niches, and ranging from parquet floor to gilt moulding, the collection is a dizzying and fragile array of priceless china. It remains a moot point whether the queen actually drank from these precious cups or indeed ate from the plates. According to reports she was practically minded, so we may assume she preferred other china for everyday use. The mirrored door on the front side of the room opens into the small chapel, the **Schloßkapelle**.

In the eastern wing take a look around the upper floor, the rococo former personal chambers of Frederick the Great, Sophie Charlotte's nephew. The **Weiße Saal** (White Room) doubled as His Highness's dining-room and his throne room. Surrounded by pink stucco marble and served at a splendidly decked table, even the humble regional meatball dish, *königsberger klopse*, is likely to have pleased the royal palate. The gem of all banqueting halls is the 42m (138ft) long **Goldene Galerie**. With its costly, gilt interior, it does justice to its name. The lower floor of this wing houses the **Galerie der Romantik**. The wretched room portrayed in one of the paintings hanging here, Karl Spitzweg's *Armer Poet* ('Poor Poet'), is in sharp contrast to the luxurious surroundings of the Schloß.

Take a brief stroll in the park to round out this royal luxury tour. Stretching down to the carp pond, the grounds are laid out in French Baroque style. Twisted ornamental flowerbeds and lopped hedges and trees are reminiscent of the gallant pastoral plays of that era. The pine avenue next to the carp pond leads to (Queen) **Königin Luise's Mausoleum**. She died over 100 years after Sophie Charlotte, in 1810. The Mausoleum which dates from 1812, was designed by Heinrich Gentz and Karl Friedrich Schinkel; the marble sarcophagus, a notable example of neoclassical sculpture, was created by Christian Daniel Rauch. Extremely popular in her own time, this monarch became such a legend after her death that, even today, female admirers decorate her grave with flowers.

Behind the carp pond, situated practically on the Spree River, the small **Teehaus Belvedere** seems tiny in comparison to the castle. In actual fact, though, this early neoclassical building is a respectable size. The display inside features a collection of porcelain manufactured by the state porcelain factory, the Staatliche Porzellanmanufaktur, during the 18th and 19th centuries. Built by C G Langhans as a tea house in 1788, the Belvedere was a frequent haunt of Frederick William II, nephew and successor of Frederick the Great, and his lover Wilhelmina Encke.

Heading back towards the castle, stroll along the Spree straight to the **Schinkel Pavilion**. Sophie Charlotte cannot have known this place, since it was not erected by Schinkel until 1824 – commissioned by gentle Luise's widower, Frederick William III. It was here that the king spent summer days with his second wife. Having holidayed in a Neapolitan villa, he had this house built in a Mediterranean style to remind him of those halcyon days. Cypresses and shimmering southern light would suit this place much better than Berlin's distinctly northern atmosphere.

Leave the castle grounds at the East Wing, and return to the present. In the **Luisen Café** (daily 7am–10pm) just opposite, you can reminisce about Queen Sophie Charlotte – whose wish to have a summer castle gave Berlin its most beautiful and lasting monument to Prussian courtly life.

Overwhelming splendour in Schloß Charlottenburg

4. A Socialist 'Disney World'

A tour of Berlin's most colourful district: 'Prenzelberg'.

–To Starting Point: U-Bahn or taxi, ask for 'Senefelder Platz'–

Glorified and discredited, innovative and run-down – this is but a small sample of the epithets which have been heaped on one small, heavily built-up workers' district in the eastern part of Berlin. **Prenzlauer Berg** still does, in fact, embody some of that spirit generally referred to as 'Old Berlin' – although not necessarily in the pretty museum sense, because the real old Berlin was full of poverty and misery. It is impossible to overlook the decaying buildings: the indifference of 19th-century city planners is apparent and visible in every street. And yet there is something lively, something unique about 'Prenzelberg', as the locals call it.

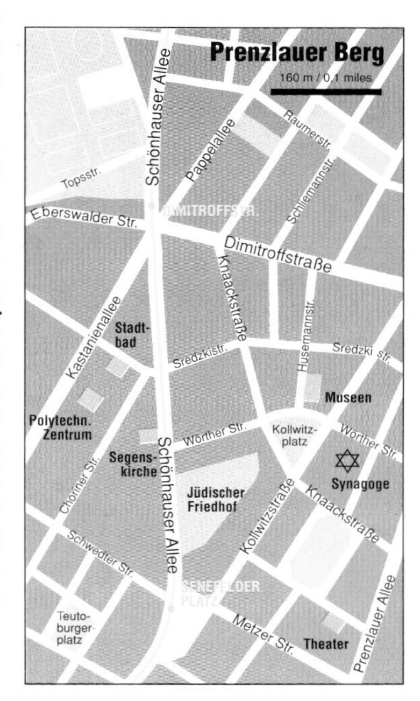

From our point of departure at the **Senefelder Platz** (square), walk up Schönhauser Allee to visit one of the oldest Jewish cemeteries, the **Jüdischer Friedhof** (Monday–Tuesday 8am–4pm). The stone inscription at the main entrance reads, 'Here you stand in silence, but when you turn around, do not remain silent' – an appeal to remember the Jews murdered by the Nazis. The words should also remind us that, even today, right-wing thugs regularly vandalise Jewish cemeteries, defiling graves. Toppled grave-

Time for a cup of coffee?

and painted swastikas are a truly oppressive sight, especially in Berlin. As in nearly all the cemeteries in the city famous names can be discovered: the publisher Leopold Ullstein and the painter Max Liebermann, for example, are buried here.

After this brief foray into Berlin's sad past, turn to the right into Wörther Straße. The tenement houses on either side are typical of Prenzelberg, with their crumbling stucco façades and cramped courtyards. The people are all busy, hurrying to get home to their flats or single-mindedly heading for Schönhauser Allee to do some shopping. At the **Kollwitzplatz** is the lively scene for which Prenzelberg is also famous: street cafés full of young people basking in the sun; children cavorting between playground, green areas and pub tables; old people suspiciously scurrying past the strangers who have streamed into this neighbourhood since the opening of the wall. The monument to the artist **Käthe Kollwitz** stares across at the strollers, a tired, bitter expression on her face. Living on nearby Knaackstraße until 1943, she found in this neighbourhood the subjects for her work, which cries out against poverty and war.

In 1987, as part of Berlin's 750th anniversary celebrations, socialist functionaries had the idea of immortalising themselves as the curators of proletarian history by setting aside a small piece of this workers' neighbourhood as an open air museum. They fixed up Husemannstraße, just off Kollwitzplatz, as an imitation of life as lived in around 1900 – or at least of how the SED Party leaders liked to believe it once was lived. The signs for the small workshops and merchants were lovingly designed and hand-lettered. The façades were restored – with material obviously not designed for eternity: the stucco has already begun to crumble. At No 12, the complex even includes a small **Museum Berliner Arbeiterleben um 1900** (Museum of Berlin Workers Around 1900; Tuesday, Thursday, Saturday 11am–6pm, Wednesday and Friday 11am–4pm). Scepticism that workers back then lived in so quaint and romantic an environment is reflected in the locals' sarcastic nickname for Husemannstraße: 'Kollywood' – ironically juxtaposing Kollwitz's grim realism and Tinseltown. At least there is one small oasis: the

Restauration 1900 (at No 1, Monday–Saturday 4pm–midnight), which serves small tasty dishes amidst 'Gründerzeit' (late 19th century industrial boom era) ambience.

Leaving this socialist 'Disney World', forge ahead into the real centre of **Prenzlauer Berg**. The spot where Dimitroffstraße runs into Schönhauserallee, and Kastanienallee into Pappel and Eberswalder Straße, is where the heart of the quarter really beats. Here the U-Bahn becomes elevated, rattling on, supported by masonry or iron pillars, towards Pankow. The tram turns the corner with an eardrum-piercing screech, while people shuffle across the traffic-filled street. And when it rains, everyone keeps their feet dry by walking on the central reservation under the elevated train, which is why this segment is called the 'Magistrate's Umbrella'. On Kastanienallee the occupied houses all compete to see which façade can don the prettiest revolutionary warpaint. Along the 'Umbrella', **Schönhauser Allee**, on the other hand, is a shopping street. The nightlife continues to pulsate vigorously, with plenty of pubs around. And if new Western commercial trends do not obliterate everything, then undoubtedly this street will remain one of the earthiest and most original in all Berlin.

Before plunging into the chaos on Schönhauser Allee, however, I recommend we first fortify ourselves with a real Berlin speciality. The Underground station U-Bahnhof Dimitroffstraße is the location of the oldest **Currywurst stand** in Berlin. The Konnopke family has been serving this obscure delicacy to passers-by since 1930, undaunted by the Nazis or the Stasi, the former East German secret police. *Currywurst*, it seems, simply transcends all political systems. And even if you are not a fast food freak, how can you possibly pass up Berlin's most historic sausage? Vegetarians, by the way, can order '*Pommes mit Mayo*'...

The 'Magistrate's Umbrella' elevated railway

5. Lübars – A Village Idyll

An excursion to a rural town: Alt-Lübars, and the Tegeler Fließ.

–To Starting Point: S-Bahn station: Waidmannslust; then Bus 20 to the final stop at Lübars; or taxi, ask for 'Alt-Lübars'–

Flying into Tegel Reinickendorf airport offers a wonderful panorama of woods and lakes that make up the greater part of this district. Reinickendorf is called the 'green north' and there is good reason for this: almost a quarter of its surface area consists of vast forest. For a country outing Berliners need not even leave the city limits. This is not a reference to those remnants of villages which have survived in some of the outlying districts, but to a real village right out in the sticks, surrounded by farms with cultivated fields, horses and chickens and two rustic village taverns. For city-dwellers for whom the surrounding countryside is too far away, **Lübars** – in northern Berlin, just behind the high-rise settlement of Märkisches Viertel – is a true oasis. In this rural spot, life seems to follow a different rhythm, with farm dogs lying about on the pavement and chickens straying off down the only street in town.

The village consists of only a few houses grouped around the small fieldstone church. The oval form of the current town goes back to its medieval layout as a 'Rundlingdorf', or nuclear village. Originally, this type of settlement had only one entrance – which is still the entrance to the village today, although the customary medieval palisade enclosure no longer exists, of course. The bus bumps along the cobblestone road and parks on the church square, the 'Kirchplatz'. Waiting to drive back, the driver passes the time chatting with one of the villagers or visitors. After all, in these simple surroundings everyone seems to know everyone else.

In the centre of the village the houses look more like town houses than farmhouses, with bits of crumbling Wilhelminian or neoclassical moulding adding a touch of modest elegance to their façades. During the last century, as the city expanded, farmers sold land, using their newly acquired wealth to build these one-storey imitations of town residences. The farmhouses around the village date back even further, some of them already extant during the 19th century. Agriculture ceased to be important here long ago, it now being more lucrative for the farmers to rent out stables and care for city-dwellers' horses. The only agriculture left involves a few oat fields harvested by tractors in the autumn.

A tour of the village involves a short walk – unless you get sidetracked at one of the two taverns. The first such danger lurks to the right in House No 8: the 'Old Village Inn', the **Alter Dorfkrug Lübars** (Wednesday–Sunday 10am–11pm), a tavern (the word 'pub' hardly seems appropriate in these rural surroundings) which looks like a backdrop from the Wilhelminian era. At the end of the village – where the road swerves sharply back towards the entrance – is the **Bündnerhaus** (No 17), a sort of co-operative house. It is one of the two buildings in Lübars which have been declared national monuments.

The building right behind it is the old school, the **Alte Schule**, which already existed in 1820. As late as the 1970s, this is where the few village children were taught. Today they are bussed to neighbouring towns. Arriving at House No 20, it is time for a rest at the village inn, literally translated as the 'Village Jug of the Merry Finch' or **Dorfkrug zum Lustigen Finken** (daily 10am–11pm) – with original Lübars country bread still baked according to an 1896 recipe, as well as some rather solid home cooking.

Village transport

The Kossätenhaus: a protected monument in Lübars

The **Kossätenhaus** – No 22, at the end of the village – is proof that not all the farmers in the region have grown wealthy. The tiny straw-thatched house, now a protected monument, used to belong to one of the *kossäten*, poor peasants who had barely enough to feed themselves. Known today as the **Schäferhütte**, the 'Shepherd's Hut', it served as the local poorhouse well into this century.

North of Lübars, with easy access via small field tracks, you will find one of the most beautiful nature reserves in all Berlin. The swampy, meadowy area, known as **Tegeler Fließ**, is all that remains of a water channel dating from the last Ice Age. A wooden walkway leads out over the watercourses branching in all directions – allowing a good look at rare fauna and flora without disturbing them in the process. This ideal is shattered, of course, when droves of strollers spoil the romantic impression – which happens almost every Sunday. Here, in the Tegeler Fließ, archaeologists have also discovered the remains of the first Berliners. Over 10,000 years ago, just before the end of the last Ice Age, reindeer hunters from the low mountain ranges far to the south met here every summer. Nowadays you can make do with the **Lustiger Finke.** This tavern may not stock any reindeer meat, but it is certainly warmer here and far more comfortable than any Ice Age hunter would ever have dreamed possible.

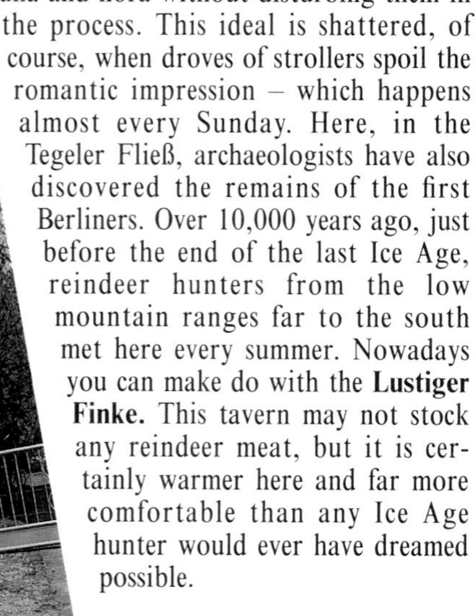

A choice of watering-holes

6. Off-Kudamm

The elegant world of the side streets off Kurfürstendamm.

–To Starting Point: U-Bahn station Spichernstraße; or taxi, ask for 'Fasanenplatz'–

Ideally, we should explore each and every one of the side streets branching off Kurfürstendamm, or the **'Kudamm'**, as it is called by the natives. There is something to see – or to buy, if your pockets are deep enough – on each of them. Everywhere you will find the flair of cosmopolitan Berlin, interspersed with a bit of Bohemia or some petty bourgeois tranquillity. The 'Off-Kudamm' itinerary upon which we are about to embark, however, covers only a small cross-section of the many lanes and by-ways. You may decide to follow my tour and, afterwards, wander according to some plan geared to your own needs or else led on by visual stimuli.

If we go by Underground (U-Bahn), then we first follow Meirottostraße along the back of the municipal theatre, the Freie Volksbühne, to Fasanenplatz. **Fasanenstraße** – an arty little lane lined with numerous galleries and boutiques – is by far the most elegant street leading off the Kudamm. If we were to continue along it we could pay **Villa Grisebach** (at No 25) a visit. This late neoclassical palace houses the **Käthe-Kollwitz Museum**. Together, the museum and gallery constitute the beginning of the 'mile of art' that stretches the entire length of Fasanenstraße. On some days one gallery 'opening' follows another, the public enjoying 'Kunst konzentriert' or 'Concentrated art'. The **Galerie Pels Leusden**, one of the most renowned in Berlin, has its rooms in the same building, offering Classical Modernism and contemporary art for sale to well-to-do art collectors from all over the world.

A good start to the day

Berlin's literary establishment meets in a Gründerzeit town house next door at No 23. The café in the **Literaturhaus**, the Wintergarten (daily 10–1am), offers a refined atmosphere as conducive to sophisticated small talk as to lofty reading. Elsewhere in the

View from the Europa-Center

building the Tucholsky Room is furnished with the renowned social satirist's furniture. The Literaturhaus also holds occasional readings which, however, rarely reflect 'Tucho's' bite or caustic wit. I would also recommend another gallery on Fasanenstraße: **Galerie Bremer** (No 37; Tuesday–Friday, noon–6pm) with modern art on display in the front rooms. And for those interested in discussing art over a glass of wine, the back room doubles as a small bar (Monday–Saturday from 8pm).

Forging ahead, eager to discover more of Off-Kudamm, turn left onto **Lietzenburger Straße**. Each day, at 7pm, the **Sperlingsgasse** – an amusement complex consisting of 13 pubs and taverns between Uhland and Knesebeck streets – opens its doors, inviting passers-by in for a 'typical Berlin nip' – in reality an atypical Berlin rip-off. You are not likely to see many locals in this establishment, but this is where the tourist buses generally unload. It is hard to imagine anything less *berlinerisch* than this pickling plant!

Now take a right turn onto **Knesebeckstraße**, a typical residential and shopping street going back to the Gründerzeit era. The lavish Wilhelminian façades and generously laid out flats with huge rooms, servants' entrances and pantries, reflect the notions of palatial living which prevailed then – and still do, for that matter. Next, we are back on the

Kudamm. There is always something going on here – 24 hours a day. Even at 3am you will still see droves of people moving up and down the pavements, marvelling at the neon signs, wanting to see and be seen. And they are not all visitors by any means. Berliners also get round-the-clock enjoyment out of their metropolitan boulevard. The bars, restaurants and discos are constantly packed and there are long queues outside the cinemas. Street-performers and musicians showing off their skills can always count on an appreciative audience. The squares, especially – Adenauer, Olivaer, Breitscheid or Joachimstaler Platz to name but a few – are focal points for the sort of colourful activity which makes many a visiting ex-Berliner homesick for Kurfürstendamm.

Turning right, enter **Bleibtreustraße**, my favourite Off-Kudamm street. The boutiques here are not exactly cheap, but they are still affordable. The crowds in the bars and restaurants are a colourful blend of elegance, tourism and the 'scene'. Here, down-to-earth consumption prevails over slick, packaged stylishness. The street's slightly grubby image has exuded a charm all its own for years: some of the exterior scenes for the 1972 movie *Cabaret* – the most

The 'water dumpling' at the Breitscheidplatz

recent screen version of Christopher Isherwood's tale of Berlin in the 1930s, *I am a Camera* – were shot here. The S-Bahn bridge, with its grime and pigeon droppings and the faded elegance of the town houses provided just the right setting. Max Reinhardt, the famous Austrian actor, director and producer, lived on Bleibtreustraße after the turn of the century, as did actress Tilla Durieux.

After turning right onto Kantstraße, we finally arrive at **Savignyplatz** – a place which does not really turn on its charm until after dark. The numerous bars, restaurants and boutiques on the side streets around the square are where the elegant and less elegant members of Berlin's party crowd like to gather. That, however, is the subject of a separate itinerary (see *Nightlife*).

7. Friedrichshain's Socialist Heritage

Along the former Stalinist boulevard to the Lenin Monument, including a turn through the Friedrichshain 'People's Park'.

–To Starting Point: U-Bahn or taxi, ask for 'Frankfurter Tor'–

When it came to constructing their capital, the communist leaders in East Berlin did not care to settle for less than their forefathers, the Prussian rulers. At the top of their list was an impressive, majestic boulevard. This meant rebuilding the old Frankfurter Allee – totally destroyed during the war – in Stalinist wedding cake style. At **Frankfurter Tor**, the former town gate, the two towers topping the massive buildings mark the beginning of our walk along **Karl-Marx-Allee**. This pompous overture is not entirely arbitrary: the towers actually mark the former site of one of the openings in the customs wall once separating Berlin from the surrounding countryside. That was over 100 years ago. Meanwhile, the street has undergone drastic change. Before the war, both sides of the street were crowded with miserable, cramped tenement houses. People reduced to living here were from the lowest levels of society. In 1945, in the Battle for Berlin, it was along this street – already an expanse of rubble as a result of the preceding months of bombing –

Lenin Platz

that the Soviet Red Army fought its way into the heart of the city.

Years later, when it was finally time to rebuild the street, the idea was not only to commemorate the Soviet liberators, but also to create totally new and, above all, spacious dwellings to fulfill the population's housing needs. Eighty metres (262ft) wide, the street is broader than Unter den Linden and lined with the same fragrant lime trees from which the latter boulevard derives its name. The buildings are vaguely reminiscent of Moscow architecture – after all, this rebuilding was intended to honour Big Brother Stalin. Although the buildings have been allowed to decay, their design is in fact, generous and full of variety. The tribute to Stalin lasted only until 1961 when the name Stalin-Allee – also mentioned in a song by the dissident bard, Wolf Biermann – was dropped. In changing it to Karl-Marx-Allee, the communist bureaucrats hoped the name would remain uncontested forever. Now who knows what name the future holds in store for the street – after all, since reunification, Marx has not had such a good press either. It was the construction workers responsible for laying this street, by the way, who gave the signal for the major uprising on 17 June 1953 – tragically quelled by uncompromising East German communist leaders backed up by Soviet tanks.

In spite of its unpleasant past, the street does have a number of charming features: wide pavements with numerous street cafés and

In the Friedrichshain Volkspark

small shops offering plenty of variety and diversion. For film fans, there are two cinemas, the Kosmos and the International, located here; lovers of Eastern European cuisine will enjoy feasting on either Hungarian food accompanied by live music at **Haus Budapest** (No 91, daily 11am–midnight) or Polish specialities at **Haus Warschau** (No 93, Sunday–Thursday 8am–12pm, Friday and Saturday 8am–3am) which includes a discothèque.

Home of Hungarian food and live music

The 'Stalin buildings' stretch as far as **Strausberger Platz** with its *wasserspiel* splashing impressively in the middle, the jets of water shimmering in multi-coloured light at night. The rest of the street is all faceless, modernistic 1960s-style architecture. Turning away with a shudder, veer right onto **Lichtenberger Straße** to find another memorial of, by and for the short-lived communist state: Lenin – a gleaming red even from afar (because of the red Ukrainian granite from which he is hewn) – gazing optimistically at the beholder from his monumental vantage point. The rest of **Lenin Platz**, the square and buildings, is of no great interest except perhaps to architects. No-one could guess back in 1970, when the statue was unveiled and the GDR was on an upturn, how deluded was the Russian revolutionary's optimism. Nor does the monument's immediate future seem rosy in the light of recent events in Moscow and Leningrad and current discussion about eliminating socialist trappings of this sort from the Berlin cityscape.

The People's Park or **Volkspark Friedrichshain**, the Tiergarten of the East, ends our ramble on a contemplative note. Revolutionary pathos resounds throughout the park – for example, in the form of the cemetery 'for those fallen in March of 1848', the **Friedhof der Märzgefallenen von 1848**. There is also a memorial dedicated to the Red Sailors, the **Rote Matrosen**, whose 1918 mutiny triggered the second – slightly more successful – German revolution. A much prettier attraction, however, awaits in the westernmost corner of the park: the **Märchenbrunnen**. This fairy tale fountain, modelled after fabled Grimm characters, was originally built for under-privileged children at the turn of the century. You can test the sharpness of your own childhood memories by seeing how many of the fairy tale figures you can recognise.

The green parks of Berlin, rather like those of Munich and London provide oases of peace in the midst of a frenetic city. No wonder they are packed in summer with young families picnicking and naturalists, both young and old, sunbathing. In the winter, frozen ponds and streams provide Breughel-like scenes as skaters waltz and children frolic on the ice.

8. Chamissoplatz and Viktoriapark

From the Marheineke Markthalle by way of Bergmannstraße and its off-beat fashions to Chamissoplatz and Viktoriapark.

–To Starting Point: U-Bahn station Gneisenaustraße; taxi, ask for 'Marheinekeplatz'–

There are still sleepy nooks to be found in Berlin – small settlements, still seemingly intact; streets where life moves along at an easy pace; with surprising oases of nature amidst the sea of buildings – even though these particular manifestations of nature required human hands to help them along.

Heading for **Marheinekeplatz** in Kreuzberg from the Underground station via Mittenwalder Straße, the visitor is immediately surrounded by the everyday hustle and bustle of the 'Kiez', or the 'district' – one of those colourful German urban working-class quarters. Renovated in turn-of-the-century style, the **Markthalle** (Market Hall) is not only the neighbourhood shopping centre, it is also a meeting place and information exchange for the local residents. The colourful array of wares – from artfully arranged mountains of fruit and vegetables, to fish and meat, all the way to costume jewellery and glittery scarves – with washing soap and scrubbing brushes thrown in as well – tempt the eye to linger and buy. In addition to the usual refreshments, the small snack stands and beer counters offer a chance to chat with the local Berliners.

There are many more opportunities to shop walking along **Bergmannstraße** on the way to Mehringdamm. Heading toward Mehringdamm on Bergmannstraße, you will find one punk store after another interspersed with the occasional off-beat fashion boutique. Here is not the place to find expensive antiques, of course, but by

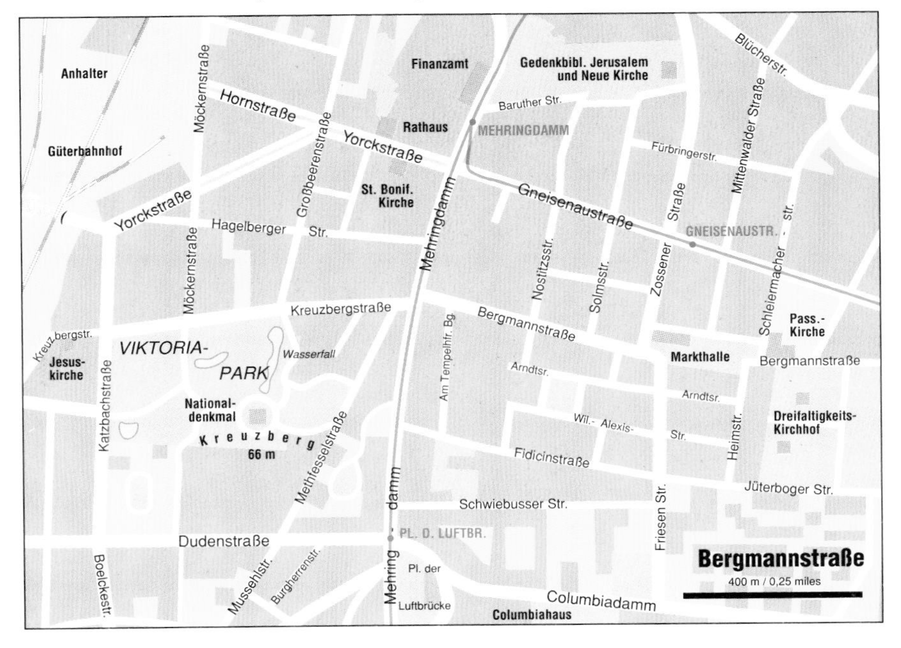

Bric a brac in Bergmannstraße

digging around amongst all the supposed junk, you may find a prize for which you would pay several times as much in one of the established second-hand stores. The merchandise in the off-beat fashion boutiques is more for young tastes: bizarre outfits just right for a ramble around Kreuzberg, or wild accessories.

Nostizstraße runs directly into **Chamissoplatz**. Here there is a nostalgic relic of 19th-century Berlin. The rectangular square with its beautifully renovated Gründerzeit buildings encloses a small green area. Restaurants like the **Chamisso** (daily 6pm–12.30am) or the Heidelberger Krug (daily 8pm–4am) are popular meeting places not only among the neighbourhood residents. And then there is also a 'Café Achteck'. This octangular 'beer disposal' facility – normally, it must be said, only at the disposal of men – is, of course, one of the famous green-painted and richly ornamented turn-of-the-century pissoirs.

Ornamental water-fountain

Back on Bergmannstraße, cross Mehringdamm and heading off to the left, make for Platz der Luftbrücke. The sculpture here – which Berliners irreverently call the 'Hunger Rake' after its shape – is a memorial to the Allied airlift during the Berlin Blockade. Continue as far as Viktoriapark which begins on Kreuzbergstraße. This is the actual **Kreuzberg**, or 'Cross Mountain', rising to an elevation of 66,000 – in millimetres, that is – with a waterfall roaring down its slope. No joke, this is a real waterfall modelled after the one in the Wolfsschlucht, a ravine in the Riesengebirge Mountains. Dating from Kaiser Wilhelm's era, it was built for 'His subjects' edification'. On hot summer days it is a popular spot for cooling scorched feet. So, clamber up the slope, scaling the 66,000-mm (216-ft) heights, to rest beside the **Nationaldenkmal** at the top. Designed by Schinkel to commemorate the wars of liberation against Napoleon, it is a popular rendezvous and vantage point today. And since the Kreuzberg is a real mountain and Berliners will stop at nothing, grapes are actually being cultivated behind the monument on the southern slope. The wine produced is really only made to be served as a 'State gift'. Instead, treat yourself to some refreshments at the **Golgatha** (daily 11am on), a huge garden restaurant. At the weekend from 10pm on, when there is a disco here, things really get jumping on the Kreuzberg.

Heading back down the northern slope admire another prize example of Wilhelminian architecture on the other side of Großbeerenstraße: **Riehmers Hofgarten**. Today this residential complex beween Hagelberger, Yorck and Großbeeren streets – built towards the end of the 19th century by a financier named Riehmer – is one of the most popular addresses in the city. The complex, with its three palatial entrances, consists of generously laid out apartments and a spacious courtyard shaded by a canopy of leafy trees. It also contains a small hotel, a restaurant and the **Kinomuseum**, which shows old films. Leaving the complex via the **Yorckstraße** exit, you will find one of the most exquisite restaurants in the area. The **Bar Centrale** (daily 5pm–3am) serves Italian *haute cuisine*, but its bistro tables also accommodate guests dropping in for just an *espresso* or a beer. It is this mix which produces its irresistibly pleasant atmosphere.

The Marheineke Markthalle

9. Spandau

A stroll through the old town of Spandau, and a visit to the Zitadelle fortress.

–To Starting Point: U-Bahn station Rathaus Spandau; or taxi, ask for 'Carl-Schurz-Straße'–

A trip to Spandau, the westernmost district in Berlin, is more of a jaunt into the surrounding Brandenburg countryside than an urban sightseeing tour. This town, you see, has more affinity to the rolling Havelland region than to the Spree marshes around Berlin. The 1920 incorporation of the town into Greater Berlin, in fact, met with concerted resistance on the part of the people of Spandau. For this reason, maintaining an identity as a discrete entity, separate from Berlin, is still very important to the locals. Never call a Spandauer a Berliner! He will be most unforgiving. Spandau, you will be told, has a more ancient history than that of the 'upstart' on the other side of the Havel.

The Spandauer Schleuse (lock)

The district is traditionally one of the largest industrial areas in Berlin. As early as the Hohenzollern era, it was here, as well as in Potsdam, that the smoking chimneys of the weapons factories began to establish Prussia's dubious fame founded on military might. The expansive industrial facilities so dominate the town's image that it is easy to forget that Spandau has quite a charming old town. At first glance, from our point of departure at **Rathaus Spandau**, the town hall, **Carl-Schurz-Straße**

would appear to be your average pedestrian precinct with the usual department stores and shops. What the metropolitan Berliner notices right away, though, is the atmosphere here. Instead of rushing along to do urgent shopping, the residents of Spandau stroll unhurriedly up and down the narrow streets, stopping to relax on one of the numerous benches, striking up conversations and enjoying the intimate, small town ambience. The building style is that of small Brandenburg Marches towns: no more than two storeys and featuring delicate scrollwork.

Reaching **Breite Straße** via Charlottenstraße, we turn left to find ourselves in front of the oldest residence in the whole of Berlin: the **Gotisches Haus**. Although simple and smooth, the façade is built of the material typical of the period: brick. Opposite the house, **Kirchgasse** takes us on a small detour to the Reformationsplatz. Walking along this narrow, romantic street is like stepping back into the Middle Ages. Dating from the 15th century, the massive Gothic church of **St Nikolai** is hemmed in by quaint, old town houses. And if you find yourself sitting at the café on the square, for example, day-dreaming about Spandau's medieval night-watchman, armed with lantern and halberd and checking to see that all is safe and sound – you are probably not dreaming. A night-watchman actually *does* still make his nightly rounds in Spandau's old town – at least during the tourist season.

After this breather, follow Breite Straße to the **Behnitz**, the oldest section of Spandau, located adjacent to the citadel. After passing the old Marienkirche, turn left onto **Kolk**, where ancient, crooked, half-timbered houses crowd along either side of the street. Newer buildings have been skilfully and seamlessly inserted here, and the Old World feel of the place remains intact. It is easy to forget here that we are still in the largest city in Germany.

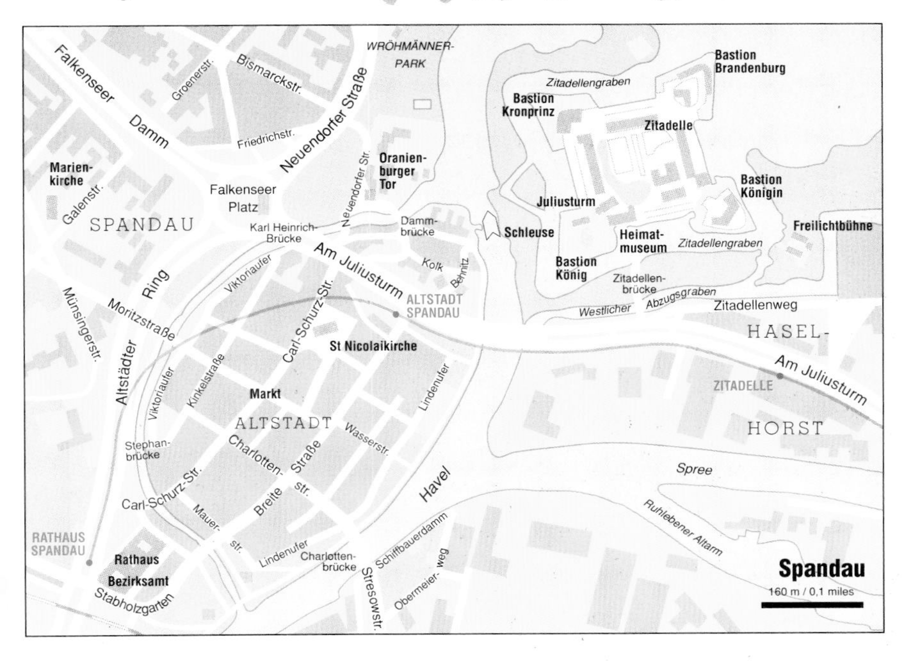

Spandau's island fortress, the Zitadelle

Proceeding on through the **Behnitz**, return to the main street where the din of the traffic threatens a return to the present. The disturbance is only temporary, however, because we are already approaching the centre of the militant Middle Ages. Once across the two bridges – first the **Havelbrücke** at **Spandauer Schleuse** (the locks), and then the **Zitadellenbrücke** – ahead is the the **Zitadelle** (citadel) itself, an island fortress which dates back to the 12th century. Massive walls surround the grounds, and the structures within the fortress include the **Heimatmuseum** (Tuesday–Sunday 10am–5pm), the local history museum displaying – among other martial implements – several huge cannonballs and a life-sized figure of a glowering guard in iron armour. The tower, the **Juliusturm**, not only looms over the entire complex, its battlement-encircled top also provides a glorious view of the old town. The top attraction here, however, is the **Zitadellenschänke** (Tuesday–Friday 6–12pm, Saturday and Sunday 11:30am onwards), a tavern with old brick-vaulted ceilings and an open fireplace, where they serve good solid medieval delicacies, and mead and beer are drunk from cattle horns. Although the foodstuffs are of decidedly 20th-century vintage, they are served up with style by neat medieval squires accompanied by ballad-singing minstrels. The aperitif with the incendiary name – *Juliusturm in Flammen*, or 'Julius Tower in Flames' – is a suitable introduction to the delicacies that follow.

Relax after a long walk

10. Köpenick on the Spree and the Dahme

The old town of Köpenick, the Schloßinsel and Kietz.

–To Starting Point: S-Bahn station Köpenick; or taxi, ask for 'Dammbrücke'–

Like Spandau, Köpenick is much older than Berlin – which naturally fills the Köpenickers with a certain pride. The small town to the south of Berlin does, in fact, still have an old town and even a castle, although it does not date back as far as the 12th century, the date when Köpenick was first mentioned. From the **Köpenick S-Bahn station**, head for the old town, or **Altstadt**, along **Bahnhofstraße** passing along the way its distinguished old houses with their crumbling façades, including a few shops catering for everyday needs. At the train station is one attraction worth a stop if you are here on the right day: Köpenick's Museum of Local History, the **Heimatkundliche Kabinett Köpenick** (Tuesday 9am–6pm). Here we can marvel at the wonders of the (local) world, some of which offer insight into the curious quirks of Köpenick humour. For example, they honour a spinster who, at the ripe old age of 80, founded a club for young men – it's simply never too late. In this tongue-in-cheek vein there are also references to the close proximity of Köpenick's former hospital and the local cemetery, as well as to the one-time location of the prison – on a street named Freiheit ('Freedom').

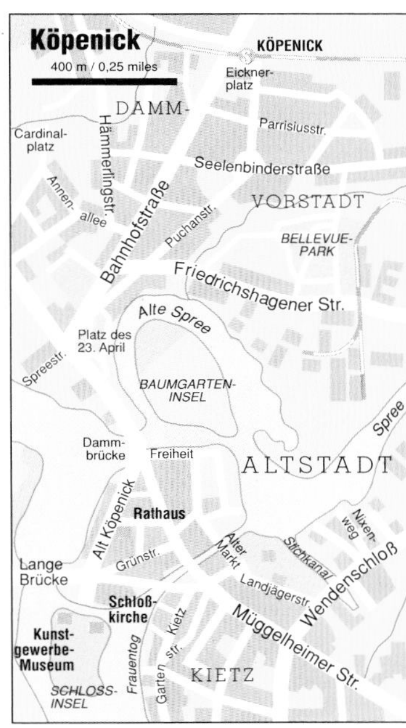

We find the first reference to the town's most famous personality, however, on the street **Alt-Köpenick**. There are still a number of buildings here dating back to the 17th century. Among them there are not only several interesting small shops, but also the brick town hall. It was in this building that the cobbler **Wilhelm Voigt**, dressed as a captain, relieved the town treasury of its contents. This crushing blow to the Prussian belief in the authority of a (Prussian) uniform is said to have set half of Germany laughing – and the other half brooding. **Carl Zuckmeyer** immortalised the poor cobbler's rich coup in his famous play, *Der Hauptmann von Köpenick*. Each year, during the last week in June, the Köpenickers commemorate the exploits of their bogus captain with a parade which heralds the opening of the town fair, the **Köpenicker Jahrmarkt**.

For some good solid cooking try the **Ratskeller** (daily 10am–11pm) located in the vaulted cellars under the **Rathaus**. The roast

Köpenick: splendour in the castle...

duck is especially recommended – or if live fowl are preferred, after (a vegetarian) dinner, take a stroll along the **Luisenhain** across the way. Although fortified with concrete, the shore along the River Spree is quite pretty. This is also where the sightseeing boats tie up, for cruises on the **Müggelsee**.

First, however, a visit to the **Schloßinsel**, or 'Castle Island', accessible only via a narrow wooden bridge. The castle is Dutch Baroque in style, and was built during the 17th century. Much earlier, however, presumably around the year 800, this site was already occupied by a Wendish castle complex. Jaxa, the Slavic king, resided here during the 12th century until he was driven off by German kings of the House of the Askanians. Today, the castle houses the **Kunstgewerbemuseum** (Wednesday–Saturday. 9am–5pm, Sunday 10am–6pm), an arts and crafts museum. The museum's richly decorated interior contrasts sharply with its relatively austere exterior. The collection housed here includes unique exibits of rare

...and rural idyll

furniture. Today, the castle chapel, with its splendid Baroque interior, serves as a concert hall, whereas the outdoor stage in the park is used for various kinds of more popular entertainment.

The castle was also the scene of a traumatic event in the personal life of Frederick the Great. It was here that the court, convening upon the orders of his father, the king, tried Frederick and his friend, Hans Herrmann von Katte – with whom he had intended to flee to England. Von Katte was condemned to death and beheaded before the prince's eyes. The crown prince himself was banished to Schloß Rheinberg. Ironically, he was far happier there than he would have been if forced to remain near his hated father.

It is now high time to take a short break at the **Schloßcafé** before continuing on into the 'Kietz'. **Grünstraße** and **Kietzer Straße**, with their old town flair and many shops, are good for a leisurely browse. In some of the shops authentic souvenirs can be picked up – a 'Hauptmann von Köpenick' rag doll, for example. For fancy dress enthusiasts, there is even a costume rental shop offering captains' uniforms complete with sabres. These days, however, do not bother trying to rob the town treasury – you'll find it empty!

A captain's uniform – on hire

The **'Kietz'** itself (the name comes from 'Chyza', which is the Slavic for 'hut') is what remains of the old fishing village of Köpenick. The sight of the roughly cobbled streets and the tiny, low houses – or 'huts' – takes us back in time. Not only do these structures actually date back some 200 years, but they have escaped the ministrations of developers and not been turned into a theme park. The small quarter still seems as poor today as the entire area once was. Here and there, however, there are signs of the first stabs at restoration: freshly whitewashed façades and colourfully painted shutters. In the good old days, by the way, it was the women here who showed their often luckless husbands how to catch fish – which is how the cove between the Schloßinsel and the Kietz got its name, **'Frauen-tog'**, or 'Women's Draught'. Neither the men nor the women do any fishing these days, though. Since those long-ago days of the feminist fisherwomen, the water quality of the Spree has deteriorated drastically, but with the new importance of the Green party and their concern with improving the environment, we can perhaps begin to hope that the pollution will one day be controlled.

11. Sanssouci Castle

The most beautiful sights in Sanssouci Park, followed by supper in Cecilienhof Castle.

–Getting There: S-Bahn station Potsdam West, then trams 1, 4 or 6 to Brandenburger Tor; or taxi, ask for 'Haupteingang Sanssouci'. To Schloß Cecilienhof take Bus F from the Sanssouci main entrance–

Für Sorgen sorgt das liebe Leben, und Sorgenbrecher sind die Reben. Goethe's homage to the soothing powers of wine translates, roughly: 'Sweet life is the maker; vines the worry-breaker.' Many years before Goethe, Frederick the Great paid tribute to this truth with walls of stone and fields of grapes. In 1744, just outside the gates of the then tiny provincial town of Potsdam – now the state capital of Brandenburg – the artistically inclined Hohenzollern king not only had the hillside terraced for a vineyard but crowned it with a small castle – which he named 'Sanssouci', or 'Without Worry'.

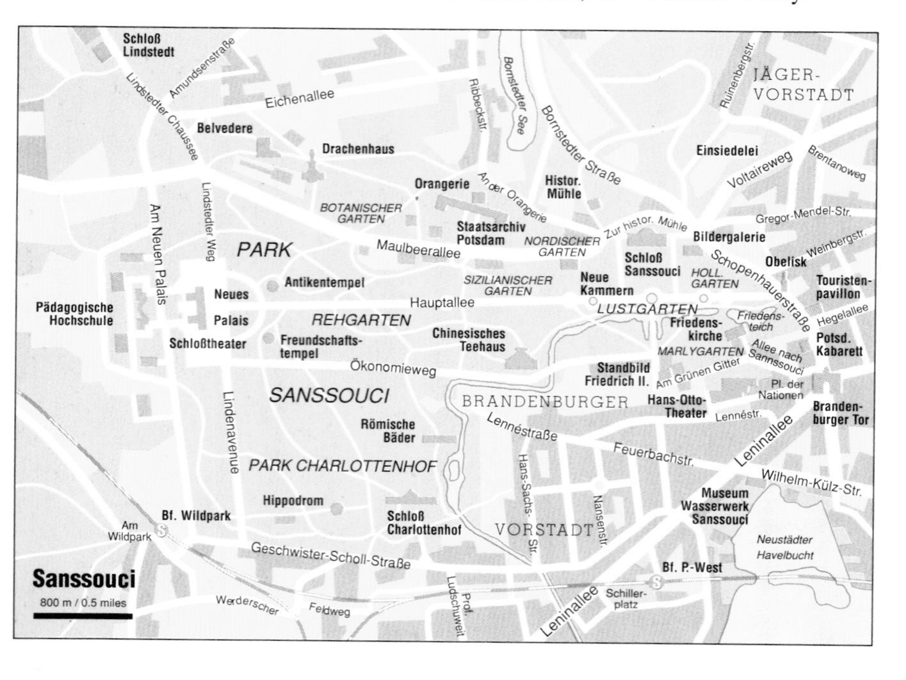

The castle 'without worry'

Whether the fruit of the vine actually dispelled his worries is not recorded. What is certain, though, is that this castle, with its 12 rooms, was Frederick's favourite residence; the retreat he escaped to in order to relax and forget the demands of ruling and representing the kingdom. In laying the cornerstone for this castle complex, Frederick 'willed' to posterity one of the most beautiful monuments on earth – now included in the official list of objects representing the cultural heritage of the world. It was his wish to be buried here with his 11 beloved greyhounds, 'without pomp, show or ceremony, by the light of a lantern without anyone following me'. However it would be another 205 years before this wish was fulfilled, in an awkward ceremony on 17 August 1991, in a Germany struggling towards unification and not a little embarassed by aspects of its Prussian military heritage.

Entering the spacious park grounds is indeed like slipping into another, ideal world. The most diverse elements of style have been combined here. Step through the obelisk portal, acknowledging the 12 marble busts with a curt nod, and turn right to face Neptune, who sits authoritatively in his grotto. With their splendid architecture, the **Bildergalerie** (Painting Gallery), behind Neptune's statue, and the **Schloß Marly**, to the left of the entrance, are both inviting sights. But the main attraction, of course, is **Sanssouci** itself – almost modestly situated above the terraces. The only thing truly modest about the building, of course, is its size. The façade and the interior design, on the other hand, represent a breathtaking display of Baroque splendour. Walking through the lovingly fur-

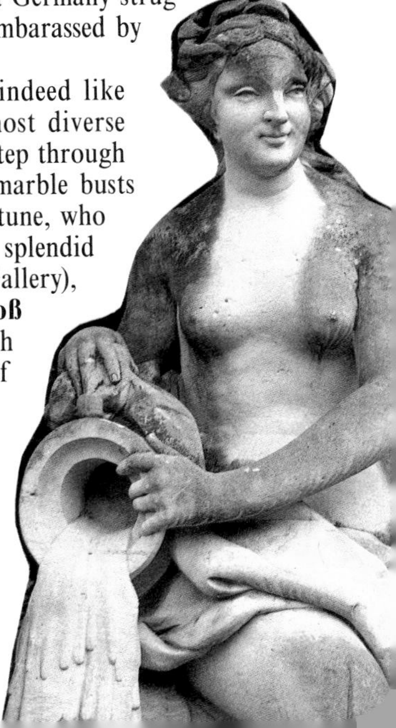

View from a distance

nished rooms, it is easy to imagine Old Fritz being kissed by the Muses – even if the results were not exactly overwhelming.

The **gardens** are no less charming and inspiring: the Dutch Garden; the Sicilian, the Nordic and the Botanical Gardens. There are numerous architectural gems scattered about the park: the Freundschaftstempel ('Temple of Friendship'), the Antikentempel, the Fasanerie ('Pheasant House'), the Hippodrom, the Römische Bäder (Roman Baths) and the **Chinesisches Teehaus**, a splendid example of delicate chinoiserie shimmering, golden, amongst the greenery of the park. **The Orangerie**, in Italian Renaissance style, rises up beyond the Maulbeerallee ('Mulberry Avenue'). Strolling down the main avenue, Hauptallee, we pass statues along the way, either gazing at the sky or looking down upon us. This is truly a promenade in its purest form.

The largest building in the park is at the end of the Hauptallee, the **Neues Palais**. Unfortunately, it has been shrouded in scaffolding for some time as the restorers have been overwhelmed trying to combat the insiduous decay with insufficient funds at their disposal.

Chinesisches Teehaus

Only some 60 of the 200 rooms can be visited at this time. One of them, the **Muschelgrotte** ('Shell Grotto'), is reminiscent of a fairy tale castle, glittering with semi-precious stones, shells and fossils. The Hohenzollerns used the castle as a 'guest house' to accommodate royal visitors in a manner befitting their station. With quarters like this, who would not have enjoyed being the king's guest?

One look at the dilapidated state of the castle complex opposite the palace is enough to break one's heart. The **Communs**, the quarters of the Royal household – once no less splendid than the palace – look as though they have been abandoned to the elements. Trees are growing out of the walls; the numerous gable figures are in danger of tumbling down – and yet the faded beauty of the building is still remarkable. It will be years before Sanssouci can be fully restored to its former splendour.

This complex was apparently not good enough for the last emperor, William II. Although World War I had already begun, he commissioned the building of yet another castle: **Cecilienhof**. Styled after an English country seat, the last Hohenzollern castle is overgrown with lush greenery. It gained most fame, however, when the Treaty of Potsdam was signed here by Truman, Attlee and Stalin on 2 August 1945, establishing the division of Germany. The conference room, including the historic round table, has been preserved to this day. A third of the building serves as a memorial; the rest was remodelled as a hotel containing one of the most expensive restaurants in Potsdam – and one with the most original menus. Trying the courses selected by Churchill (swallow's nest soup, breast of turkey and whisky cream), Truman (rosetta of ham on Waldorf salad, tournedos Boston and pineapple *parfait*) and Stalin (Ukra fish soup, glazed ham and honey nut *parfait*) makes for an interesting dining experience.

Statues at the Chinesisches Teehaus

12. Chorin Monastery

Excursion to the 13th-century 'Redbrick Gothic' Kloster Chorin.

–Getting There: By car: from the Berliner Ring take the Szczecin Autobahn, exit at Eberswalde-Finow, proceed towards Angermünde to the turn-off to the Kloster (approximately 1 hour). By train: S-Bahn to Bernau, then the Stralsund train to 'Chorin-Kloster'–

About 9km (5 miles) north of Eberswalde-Finow, situated in the middle of nowhere, is a massive monastic ruin which towers above all other sacred buildings in the surrounding region. **Kloster Chorin** has not been used as a working monastery for centuries, however. During the GDR era, it was one of the regime's showpieces, and for good reason: the powers-that-were liked to show off their successes and, in the case of Kloster Chorin, their restoration work truly was a unique achivement, but more on this subject later.

In Kloster Chorin

From the station, set out on foot through a beech wood, one of those wonderful forests of the Brandenburg Marches which big-city dwellers simply cannot get enough of. Or, arriving by car, park in the open area a short distance from the cloister. It is surprising not to find a paved car park at such a tourist attraction – it almost seems to have been created by accident. Nor are there the usual tourist-orientated souvenir stands or hectic catering services, but this is precisely what makes the monastery so charming. Gothic architecture, especially the brick variety, has something inherently gloomy about it. This melancholy, and its shroud of mystery are, of course, what gave the word 'gothic' its original connotations of horror. Were these not the sinister vaults in whose monastic solitude horrible deeds were committed? Where degenerate aristocrats ruined themselves labouring under delusions of their own uniqueness? Walls inside whose secret rooms Dr Frankenstein created his artificial human being? Where manuscripts were stored recording arcane truths? Where the abbot reigned supreme, torturing his monks in his excess of religious frenzy, or perhaps, secretly seducing simple peasant girls by instilling in them terrible feelings of guilt? Enough of these fantasies! But I do confess that each time I enter

Impressive brickwork...

this old monastery, all of these sinister connotations come to my mind. However, if truth be known, Chorin's documented history is much more prosaic.

The building was constructed by Cistercian monks during the 13th century. Rejecting the Romanesque style, they decided in favour of more modern architecture, which at that time meant Gothic. Constructed using local building materials, Chorin became the precursor and model of all the so-called 'Backsteingotik' ('Redbrick Gothic') buildings. The monks here hardly lived lives of pious self-sacrifice. As was usual at the time, they owned most of the surrounding region. Some 20 towns such as Sandkrug and Niederfinow were under their control. They had an absolute monopoly on all vital activities. No-one was even allowed to bake bread without their permission. The hard work of which the monks liked to boast was, of course, performed by God-fearing peasant lads intent on *becoming* monks. The friars themselves performed the intellectual and or spiritual work, supposedly for the common good – but always for their own benefit, of course. (Perhaps my earlier ruminations on the Gothic were not so far-fetched, after all.) During the Reformation, however, these devout and not-so-devout governors of land and souls were banished by the incensed populace. But it was not the new attitude represented by

...and startling views

Martin Luther which caused the people to revolt; it was chiefly their own oppression at the hands of the almighty Catholic Church – with its marked interest in (profitable) worldly affairs. Ever since the 16th century, the area's inhabitants have used the monastery to stable their animals and as a 'stone quarry'. One cannot blame them for this secular desecration, and yet it has meant the destruction of one of the most impressive works of the Early Gothic period. It was not until the 19th century – when it became acceptable to recall the catholic and medieval heritage – that reconstruction got under way. And the former and admittedly atheistic GDR deserves the credit for this latest chapter in the building's rejuvenation, for the work was carried out with the utmost care.

The former kitchen

New bricks were fired according to the old-fashioned method; not simply stuck together using modern chemical binding agents, but with the traditional egg white – or so the restorer assures me. The popular wisdom that egg white and liverwurst make the best glue – which does not say much for the latter's nutritional qualities – was given credence here. And, in fact, except for the southern aisle, which was totally razed by post-Reformation peasants, the renovated walls look as though they have been restored to their original condition and all their rosy redbrick glory. Within this austere monastery, with its pointed arches, it seems as if the steps of the monks can still be heard. Sensitive visitors are most impressed by the sacristy. The monks' cells still evoke a sense of the lofty monastic principles of poverty and renunciation, and one look at the cavernous kitchen gives you a good idea of where the term 'frugal meal' originally came from.

But the most marvellous atmosphere of all is evoked during the **open air concerts** in summer and I would encourage you to try and schedule your excursion to Kloster Chorin to coincide with one of these events (for information, contact the town administration, or 'Gemeindeverwaltung', in Chorin; Tel: 336). On these occasions, classical music is performed inside the old church nave, by ensembles such as the Staatskapelle Dresden. The audience sits in the grass-covered courtyard looking towards the monastery, listening to the music and, at these times, any lingering thoughts of ruthless abbots and Dr Frankenstein are laid to rest.

13. Water and Woods: The Spreewald

Punting through one of the most beautiful landscapes in Europe.

–Getting There: By car: via the intersection Schönefelder Kreuz on the Dresden Autobahn to the Forst turn-off, then the first exit to Lübbenau (around 1½ hours). By train: towards Cottbus or Görlitz–

My claim that this itinerary covers one of the 'most beautiful landscapes in Europe' is, naturally, very subjective. But as a West Berliner I am always amazed what gems we have right on our doorstep, so to speak. Forget Florida: with its meadows and rain forest, swamps, reeds and watercourses branching out in all directions, the **Spreewald** is much more beautiful. Granted, the climatic conditions are very different, but the Spreewald is, for Berliners, a stone's throw away.

Despite the tourist boom, a **boat trip** around the Spreewald remains a bit of an adventure. **Lübbenau**, the self-styled 'Gate to the Spreewald', is where most of the punts are booked. If you can avoid the weekend, you will even find a seat without having to queue. And then we are off, for a close encounter with nature! With slow, deliberate movements the punter poles the boat forward through the sluggishly flowing water, sending it gliding between small islands and through a jungle of alder and birch trees. Here, everything looks strange and exotic. In

Jolly boating weather…

spring and autumn, with everything shrouded in a veil of mist, the landscape takes on an eerie quality. (Students of German literature may be reminded of the sinister setting in Goethe's *Erlkönig*: 'Look, Father, do you not see the Erlkönig?') Grass snakes rustle on the bank, a cuckoo calls out, grey herons or kingfishers suddenly rise from the surface of the water. If you are lucky you may even spot an otter. There is a sort of quiet which one only encounters in the wild – and which is also incredibly soothing. There is not a trace to be seen of the coal mining industry located nearby, not a sound to be heard of bustling 20th-century civilisation.

Meadows and pastures appear at the water's edge, and through the bushes along the shore there are glimpses of isolated log cabins with thatched roofs and colourful gardens. Storks have built their

Punting in Berlin

nests in the thatch, and some of the gables are adorned with the figure of the 'Schlangenkönig', the legendary Snake King of Sorbian legend. In late summer, the locals offer their guests the regional culinary speciality: pickled gherkins – the best I've ever eaten. (My enthusiasm, however, may be due primarily to the setting in which I ate them.) This is also where the famous *Spreewälder Leinöl* (linseed oil) comes from – a delicacy with new potatoes, although the pungent flavour is not to everybody's liking.

The trip to **Lehde** takes about two hours. The **'Hochwald Rundfahrt'**, a tour through the older forest to Leipe and then back to Lübbenau takes anything from eight to 10 hours, including stops for lunch and coffee. Naturally, it is also possible to rent a canoe and set out on your own, but you should take care not to lose your way in the jungle-like forest. For the adventuresome, however, this sort of tour is an unforgettable experience. Although shorter, the trip to Lehde is worthwhile for the additional attractions awaiting you there. The lagoon village features an outdoor museum, the **Freiland-Museum** (May–October: daily except Monday), complete with dwellings, punt sheds, stables and displays of farming implements and household equipment. The tiny homes convey an impression of how the modest Sorbs lived.

These original Slav inhabitants of the area settled here over 1,000 years ago. They did not assimilate until the Middle Ages when forced to do so by the Franks and Germans. They have nevertheless managed to preserve their own autonomous culture in south-east Germany – often in defiance of their rulers. The ferry-people, particularly the women, still occasionally wear their traditional costumes with starched bonnets and frilly blouses – and the demotic Sorbian language is becoming increasingly popular as a sign of their strong sense of ethnic identity.

In Lehde, the most historic restaurant is the 'Jolly Sturgeon', or **Fröhliche Hecht** (May–September daily 8am–8pm; October–April Wednesday–Friday 4–11pm, Saturday 11am–midnight, Sunday 11am–5pm). Another tourist restaurant, the once elegant **Waldhotel Wotschofska** (May–September Wednesday–Monday 9am–5pm) features specialities such as *Karpfen in Lebkuchensoße* ('carp in gingerbread sauce'). Both restaurants are located along the punting tour route and generally serve as stops. Here too it is a good idea to avoid the weekends, when conditions are crowded and the quality of the food suffers from the production-line service.

Returning first to Lübbenau and, from there, to Berlin, memories of our Spreewald excursion seem like a dream – confirming my promise that the Spreewald is, in fact, one of the most beautiful landscapes in Europe.

A fairytale setting

14. The In-Crowd and Bohemian Savignyplatz

Supper and people-watching after dark on Savignyplatz; then bar hopping into the wee hours among bohemians, VIPs and wannabes.

–To Starting Point: S-Bahn or taxi, ask for 'Savignyplatz'–

'The great thing about Berlin,' my guests from the former 'Wessiland' (West Germany) tell me, 'the truly unique feature, is the length of the nights.' So, where are we headed tonight, for it is time once again to make a night of it, have a ball, only to struggle out of bed the next morning, or rather, the next afternoon – still bushed. Here are some good places to try.

Mirror, mirror on the wall…

Anyone who wants to experience a little of Berlin's after-dark bohemian scene, and perhaps rub elbows with the in-crowd, should head for **Savignyplatz**. Start with supper at the **Paris-Bar** (Kantstraße 152; closed Sunday), a very popular French bistro. Even the snooty waiters in their long aprons are essential elements of this place's unique style. During the February film festival do not even bother looking for a table here, the place will be packed. Everybody even remotely involved in cinema shows up here during the festival, pecking cheeks and doing everything they can to remain conspicuously incognito. The food, although good, is nothing to write home about, but then food is not what the Paris-Bar is all about. It's who's-who-and-here that matters, though anyone found ogling will be treated with contempt. The best approach is to pretend you just got the lead in the new Chabrol film – and let the others stare.

Tête-à-tête in the Café Savigny

The **Café Hegel** (Savignyplatz 2) is more informal. The décor consists of white walls festooned with modern art. As the Russian publican pours a vodka it is surprising to notice that the bookshelves along one wall contain the collected works of Hegel. Tired singers from the Deutschen Oper and melancholy Russians in exile round out the philosophical atmosphere.

VIPs who like to flaunt their celebrity more discreetly prefer to withdraw to the **Florian** (Grolmannstraße 52). Here, among peers, you stick to your small insider group and drink your beer at the bar or sip champagne at linen-covered tables. You may see the editor of a small independent publishing house discussing final changes in a manuscript with its author, or a French movie star spooning down his soup after a hard day on the set, while the as-yet-unknown painter at the next table studies the walls trying to decide whether they would be suitable for hanging her work. Taking a cue, simply pretend to be here on important, private business.

Too quiet for you here? No problem: the **Café Savigny** (Grolmannstraße 53) is right next door, a small, cool espresso bar where you can act as wild and wacky as you like, providing you manage to grab a free table. Here, too, you may see many a well-known face, only they do not stand out at all among the unknown ones, for at the Savigny everyone is a star. Here, the Bleibtreustraße boutique-owner is modelling her latest creation in flaming colours. At another table, a journalist-cum-perpetual-failure has his pretty new acquaintance pinned down with a detailed description of the 'novel-of-the-century' which he has been intending to write for 15 years. The voluptuous Italian waitress has shown up today with a hair-do which would have made Madame Pompadour green with envy – in fact, it's a miracle she clears the spotlights on the ceiling with it. Less noisy, the chairs and tables outside are resting places for the foot-weary. Here, you can watch passers-by brooding over the question of where to spend the evening. Or, as the night wears on, you may find yourself gazing into the eyes of the person across the table, wondering where you will be spending the rest of night.

Cabaret

Let us now cast a glance inside **Carmer's** (Carmerstraße 2) for a glimpse of blow-dried pop stars; socialites craving admiration and advertising their car-key-jangling importance, laughing loudly at the latest show-biz anecdotes; business-people talking earnestly and collecting their expense account bills – although it is not clear what business it is they have to account for.

Things are a bit cosier at **Diener** (Grolmannstraße 47). Founded in the 1950s by Franz Diener, the former German middle-weight boxing champion, this 'diner' does not seem to have changed one bit since those days. The yellowing walls are covered with the mementoes of an athletic career; with fading film posters of yesteryear giving the place a touch of authenticity – all reminders of the faded glory of stars in the 'good old days'. Billy Wilder, director of *Sunset Boulevard* and *Some Like it Hot*, is said to have dined here, and there is a persistent rumour that the late German New-Wave film director Rainer Werner Fassbinder's charismatic presence once caused a stir here. This is one of the nerve centres where theatre people and journalists meet to forge that fertile alliance which guarantees crowded gossip columns.

As the sky begins to brighten on the horizon, accentuating the darkening shadows under our eyes, we head for home. After all, tomorrow night in Berlin will prove just as lengthy and eventful.

15. Wild and Woolly 'Kreuzbergistan'

Hearty or international dining, making the rounds of the 'Kreuzberg' pub scene, and dancing till dawn.

–Getting There: S-Bahn to Maritzplatz;
or taxi, ask for 'Oranienenstraße'–

Start off at Oranienplatz in the heart of Kreuzberg with a proper meal at **Max & Moritz** (Oranienstraße 162). This historic restaurant has been serving good solid Berlin cooking for ages: *Eisbein* (boiled knuckle of pork) or *Hoppelpoppel* (if you are curious to know what this is, you will just have to give it a try) with chips. It's just the sort of fare to keep you full for a while and line your stomach for the night ahead. Full and satisfied, all we have to do now is move a few doors down to the **Anton** (Oranienstraße 170).

During the day it is very bright and friendly here but, after dark, 'O-Straße' – as abbreviation-mad Berliners call the street – grows livelier. The dedicated cyclist unclips his jean cuffs, takes off his hand-knitted jumper and starts distributing leaflets for the 'Green Cyclists'. A punk trudges in, circling the crowded tables, jingling a coffee tin and soliciting donations for the 'jail fund'. The neighbourhood social worker pops in with a couple of colleagues for a fortifying beer before starting another night of devoted work. The student in the corner hopes she will finally find time to read the *taz*, Berlin's leftist/anarchist/green newspaper – no small feat here, considering the decibels generated by conversation and music.

The **Dörti** (Oranienstraße 169) offers us our first taste of the real Kreuzberg pub scene. The joint is cramped, stuffy and unconventional – just the way a pub should be. Many among the clientèle at the bar, either lost in thought or engrossed in conversations of terrible importance, may have actually dreamt of revolution back in the 1960s. Today, conversation generally centres more around the 'plight of the Left', the failure of 'the socialists next door', and the all-round loss of Utopias.

At a later hour, pop over to **Sox** (Oranienstraße 39), as there is no point in showing up at a disco before 11pm. The good thing about Sox is that there is no dress or face check at the door. With its sober black interior the club serves one purpose only: dancing. And everyone is welcome to join in. The clientèle is a colourful mixture mostly dominated by local residents of the district, the 'Oranien-Kiez' and the place still retains some of the old 'Wall border-zone' atmosphere.

Heinrichplatz is the wild heart of Kreuzberg – even though this wildness lives on primarily in the memories of seasoned street

Relax and drink at Max & Moritz

fighters. The area still looks as messy as ever, with everything looking anarchic and run-down. But 'all ye who enter here' need have no fear. True this is where the fiercest street-fighting took place in the 1980s, but it has long since become legend and all's quiet on the Kreuzberg front. The quarter's watering hole is the **Elefant** (Oranienstraße 12), and the crowd here is not the militant one which makes the evening news, but the normal, laid back people who actually inhabit the neighbourhood. The place is always packed, the atmosphere just below boiling point. Here you can natter with Tom, Dick and Mary, discuss world politics or the housing problem, and make the best of friends – for one night. Regulars profess that Manfred Krug – a movie star who left East Germany years ago – has been here a number of times to shoot scenes for his TV series *Liebling Kreuzberg*.

The **Rote Harfe** ('Red Harp') right next door (Oranienstraße 13) is another establishment which never really changes – despite the various renovation efforts. Kreuzbergers will tell you the pub has been around forever. This is where Kreuzberg interfaces with the rest of the world. The 'Harfe' has the best 'box seats' for demos and happenings, and locals can sit by the window, comment on the events on Heinrichplatz, and be on top of things without really getting involved.

The **Café Jenseits**, a bit further along, is brighter and more cheerful – especially at night when the regular clientèle livens the place up. After all, Kreuzbergers are always a bit faster off the mark, more on the ball, more aggressive than other Berliners. Moving on from here, cross Skalitzer Straße and plunge into the quintessential alternative cultural scene. The **Madonna** (Wiener Straße 22) epitomizes Kreuzberger nightlife. The ambience is as raw

Shrill colours in the windows

and unrefined as the people are unconventional and lively. Anyone showing up here in a tuxedo or a silk evening gown would stand out as an eccentric. The carefully styled punks make for a lively contrast with those wearing grease-stained overalls. Smugly gesturing youngsters flash and preen – leaning against the same stand-up tables as the dispirited boozers. The music makes it hard to talk, and yet they all seem absorbed in conversation. If you are interested in conversation, you are better off next door at the **Panama** (Wiener Straße 23) where, despite the garish interior, it is a bit quieter.

The rest of the night is reserved for the **Bronx**, a disco which truly does the New York slum credit. The unpretentious atmosphere is characterized by dilapidated masonry and heavy iron doors, and the kind of music which will make you shake a leg in no time flat. A no-nonsense atmosphere prevails, everyone intent on pleasure.

SEIT
1872
Berliner
Kindl
Das Pils nach guter alter Art
1/2 l 3.-
1.-

Shopping

As far as shopping is concerned, you can get anything you want in Berlin, from the most horrific kitsch to the finest works of art; from everyday essentials to outré extravaganzas. It goes without saying that the availability of consumer goods is still the biggest difference between East and West

Warm clothes for cold days

Berlin – but the East Berliners are gradually catching up. Not only are Western retailers opening branches in the eastern part of the city; the 'Easterners' themselves are creating a shopping culture all their own, with a variety of new, original products.

Traditionally, the best shops for all types of merchandise have been located along the **Kurfürstendamm** and its side streets. These, together with other shopping streets scattered throughout the city, provide a wonderful opportunity for an extensive shopping tour.

The ultimate consumer emporium is, of course, the **'KaDeWe'** – short for **Kaufhaus des Westens** ('Department Store of the West') – at Wittenbergplatz. This exclusive department store offers just about every sort of merchandise imaginable – all arranged in tasteful displays. The famous sixth floor – the food department – is particularly worth seeing. It probably even beats Cockaigne, the proverbial land of milk and honey. Hundreds of types of sausage and cheese – just to mention the more mundane foodstuffs – are stocked next to the finest delicacies from all over the world. All the top *hautes couturiers* are represented in the store as well, but you will also find a wide range of ordinary ready-to-wear brand-name clothing. And none of these luxury goods is really any more expensive here than in speciality shops. For an interesting mix of boutiques, entertainment venues and pubs, try the **Europa-Center** at Breitscheidplatz or the **Kudamm-Ecke** at the intersection of the Kurfürstendamm and Joachimsthaler Straße.

If poking around in second-hand and antique shops is your cup of tea, **Suarezstraße** and **Bergmannstraße** (in Kreuzberg) provide the ultimate tea party. On Suarezstraße, as well as on the side streets, Pestalozzi and Schillerstraße, more up-market junk and antiques are to be found, whereas on Bergmannstraße, there are more everyday objects, and even small gems to be discovered hidden beneath mounds of junk. The weekends are flea market (*Flohmarkt*) time (Saturday and Sunday 8am–3pm) – the most popular one being on **Straße des 17 Juni** at the Bahnhof Tiergarten. Often you will find better bargains at the smaller markets on **Reichpietschufer** near the Anhalter Bahnhof or on **Humboldthain** in Wedding, since the stands are run mainly by individuals rather than by professional dealers.

Bedtime reading

For a foray into the disappearing world of ex-GDR industrial products and consumer culture, the flea market at **Arkonaplatz** in Prenzlauer Berg is just the place. Here you can turn up many an odd item or occasional piece of drollery.

For art fans, I recommend **Fasanenstraße** – among experts it is considered *the* gallery lane. Wilmersdorfer Straße (Charlottenburg) and Schloßstraße (Steglitz) are unadulterated shopping streets, department stores interspersed with speciality shops. Kantstraße (Charlottenburg) between Amtsgerichtsplatz and Savignyplatz is more interesting, however, with boutiques, restaurants and pubs, and shops selling exotic and everyday items lining both sides. The new merchandising culture in the eastern part of the city is developing primarily along **Unter den Linden** – and this boulevard is shaping up as serious competition for the Kurfürstendamm. Schönhauser Allee, Karl-Liebknecht Straße, Rathausstraße and Friedrichstraße are all worth visiting, even if buying is not the main object – it is almost as much fun to window-shop here.

Fashion Boutiques

Durchbruch
Schlüterstraße 54, Charlottenburg.
Avant garde clothing à la New York.

Halloween
Suarezstraße 62, Charlottenburg.
Hallucenogenic London fashions.

Lilas
Bleibtreustraße 47, Charlottenburg.
Velvet, silk and other precious fabrics, creatively interpreted.

Maria Makkaroni
Bleibtreustraße 49, Charlottenburg.
Second-hand and artfully distressed designs.

Kaufhaus Schrill
Bleibtreustraße 46, Charlottenburg.
Just what the name promises: 'strident' and 'offbeat'.

Schwarzmarkt
Grunewaldstraße 91, Schöneberg.
Paint it (all) black: leather, patent leather and latex.

Horn
Kurfürstendamm 213, Wilmersdorf.
Elegant evening wear.

Kramberg,
Kurfürstendamm 56-57, Wilmersdorf.
Italian designer fashions.

Ellmodes
Dimitroffstraße 10, Prenzlauer Berg.
Ladies' hats.

Kostümhaus
Veteranenstraße 27, Mitte.
Designer wear for the courageous.

Norberts
Bleibtreustraße 24, Wilmersdorf.
The city's most fashionable boutique for best-dressed men.

Vincente
Wilmersdorfer Straße 107a, Charlottenburg.
The individual touch for men.

Luxury Accessories

Les Dessous
Fasanenstraße 42, Wilmersdorf.
Luxury lingerie.

Nouvelle Wäscheboutique
Bleibtreustraße 24, Wilmersdorf.
Luxury articles for the bedroom.

Fasetti
Bleibtreustraße 24, Wilmersdorf.
Sophisticated leatherwear.

Münich & Wagner
Wielandstraße 13, Charlottenburg.
Exclusive men's jewellery.

Cartier
Fasanenstraße 28, Wilmersdorf.
Luxury items from Cartier.

Misfit Boots
Kantstraße 28, Charlottenburg.
Footwear for the urban cowboy.

Mekkanische Rose
Leibnizstraße 47, Charlottenburg.
Oriental palace of all things aromatic.

Harry Lehmann
Kantstraße 106, Charlottenburg.
A concoct-it-yourself perfumery.

Knopf Paul
Zossener Straße 10, Kreuzberg.
A fabulous button emporium.

Toc
Mommsenstraße 4, Wilmersdorf.
Extravagant fashion jewellery.

Ambiente am gedeckten Tisch
Passauer Straße 36, Schöneberg.
Precious tableware.

Art Deco Astoria
Bleibtreustraße 50–50a, Charlottenburg.
Art deco accessories and copies.

Rügge
Kurfürstendamm 73, Wilmersdorf.
Up-market gifts.

Charivari
Preußenallee 39, Charlottenburg.
A priceless collection – from frilly frocks to small objets d'art.

Gombert Christal
Kurfürstendamm 41, Wilmersdorf.
Fine crystal.

Speciality Shops

Ararat
Schlüterstraße 12, Charlottenburg.
Collectible postcards.

Grand Hand
Marx-Engels-Forum 19, Mitte.
Cards from the Altenburg card factory.

Ballonshop
Gloria-Galerie, Kurfürstendamm 13, Charlottenburg.
Balloons, in more than 99 variations.

Il Cacto
Kantstraße 23, Charlottenburg.
Cacti unlimited.

Take off
Langenscheidtstraße 7, Schöneberg.
Weird and wonderful novelties.

Meißener Porzellan
Unter den Linden 38b, Mitte.
Creations in Meißener porcelain.

KPM
Kurfürstendamm 205, Wilmersdorf.
Royal Prussian porcelain.

Zauberladen
Greifswalder Straße 197, Prenzlauer Berg.
Magic for magicians.

Lichtblick-Lampen
Knobelsdorffstraße 23, Charlottenburg.
Monday–Friday 3–6pm,
Beautiful old lamps.

Booksellers

Autorenbuchhandlung
Carmerstraße 10, Charlottenburg.
Authors' readings a speciality.

Bücherbogen
Savignyplatz, Charlottenburg.
Art, design and film books.

Grober Unfug
Zossener Straße 32/33, Kreuzberg.
Comics and cartoons.

Kommedia
Potsdamer Straße 131, Schöneberg.
Media and computer titles.

Lilith
Charlottenburg, Knesebeckstraße 86.
Women's and feminist literature.

Morgenwelt
Körtestraße 27, Kreuzberg.
Science fiction and fantasy.

Prinz Eisenherz
Bleibtreustraße 52, Charlottenburg.
Gay literature.

Rauchzeichen
Vorbergstraße 9, Schöneberg.
Dada and anarchist.

Schikowski
Motzstraße 30, Schöneberg.
Occult and esoteric.

Schropp
Potsdamer Straße 100, Schöneberg.
Foreign language and travel titles.

Music

Musikhaus Carl Friedrich Zelter
Spandauer Straße 29, Mitte.
Sheet music and books.

Canzone
Savignyplatz 5, Charlottenburg.
Ethnic music and songs.

Mr Dead & Mrs Free
Bülowstraße 5, Schöneberg.
Independent and imported labels.

Bote & Bock
Europa-Center.
There is no vinyl, CD or cassette that you cannot find here.

Jazzcock
Behaimstraße 4, Charlottenburg.
Jazz.

Twang-Tone
Frankenstraße 2, Schöneberg.
Weird, second-hand rarities here.

Art Galleries

Avantgarde-Galerie
Leibnizstraße 60, Charlottenburg.
Tel: 3247823.
Monday–Friday 2–6.30pm.

Galerie Brusberg
Kurfürstendamm 213, Wilmersdorf.
Tel: 8827682.
Tuesday–Friday 10am–1pm, 2.30–6.30pm; Saturday 10am–2pm.

Endart Galerie
Oranienstraße 36, Kreuzberg.
Tel: 653317.
Monday–Sunday 4–10pm.

DAAD Galerie
Schöneberg, Kurfürstenstraße 58.
Tel: 2613640.
Daily 12.30pm–7pm.

Galerie Anselm Dreher
Pfalzburger Straße 80, Wilmersdorf.
Tel: 8835249.
Tuesday–Friday 2–6.30pm,
Saturday 11am–2pm.

Elefanten Press Galerie
Oranienstraße 25, Kreuzberg.
Tel: 650051.
Monday–Saturday 10am–6.30pm,
Sunday 1–6pm.

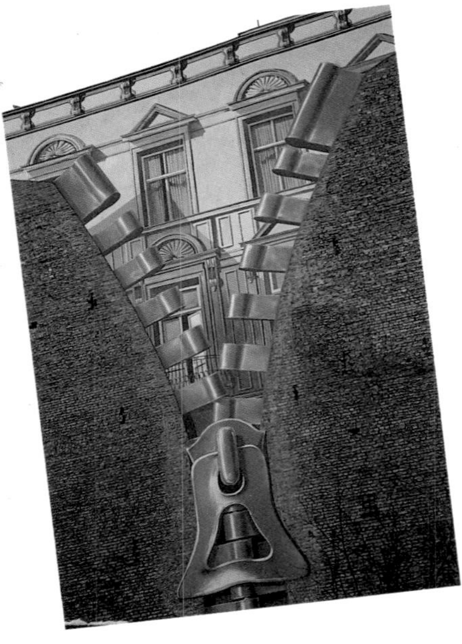

Raab Galerie
Potsdamer Straße 58, Schöneberg.
Tel: 2619217.
Monday–Friday 10am–6.30pm,
Saturday 10am–2pm.

Galerie Springer
Fasanenstraße 13, Charlottenburg.
Tel: 3121042.
Tuesday–Friday 2–7pm,
Saturday 11am–2pm.

Zwinger Galerie
Dresdener Straße 125, Kreuzberg.
Tel: 654605.
Tuesday–Friday 3–7pm,
Saturday 11am–2pm.

Galerie Art Acker
Ackerstrasse 18, Mitte.
Tel: 2826314.
Daily 9am–5pm.

Galerie A
Strausberger Platz 4, Friedrichshain.
Tel: 4375832.
Monday–Friday 10am–6pm.

Galerie im Dreieck
Oderberger Straße 6, Prenzlauer Berg.
Thursday–Sunday 3–7pm.

Galerie im Turm
Frankfurter Tor 1, Friedrichshain.
Tel: 5880400.
Tuesday–Saturday 11am–3pm, 4–7pm.

Galerie Weißer Elefant
Almstadtstraße 11, Mitte.
Tel: 2823908.
Tuesday–Friday 11am–7pm,
Saturday 3–6pm.

Galerie Wohnmaschine
Tucholskystraße 36, Mitte.
Tel: 2815812.
Wednesday 5–7pm, Sunday 3–7pm.

Design Galleries

Berlinetta Industrial Design
Oranienplatz 4, Kreuzberg.
Tel: 6141150.

Berliner Zimmer
Clausewitzstraße 1, Charlottenburg.
Tel: 8826215.

Design-Galerie
Wielandstraße 37, Charlottenburg.
Tel: 3248984.
Monday–Friday 3–6.30pm,
Saturday 11am–2pm.

Design-Transfer-Galerie
Grolmannstraße 16,
Charlottenburg.
Tel: 3138082.

Internationales Design-Zentrum (idz)
Wielandstraße 31, Charlottenburg.
Tel: 8823051.
Monday–Friday 10am–6pm.

Photography Galleries

Eylau 5
Eylauer Straße 5, Kreuzberg.
Tel: 7863024.
Tuesday and Thursday 4–7pm.

Bilderladen Fokus
Dahlmannstraße 5, Charlottenburg.
Tel: 3925943.
Wednesday–Friday 4–7pm, Saturday 11am–2pm.

Galerie Nagel
Fasanenstraße 42, Wilmersdorf.
Tel: 8821890.
Monday–Friday noon–6.30pm, Saturday 11am–2pm.

Werkstatt für Fotografie
Friedrichstraße 210, Kreuzberg.
Tel: 25883426.
Monday–Friday 5–9pm.

Details are published in the magazines *Tip* and *Zitty*, and in newspapers.

Fine Wines and Spirits

Enoteca
Holsteinische Straße 22, Wilmersdorf.
Tuesday–Thursday 3–6.30pm,
Friday 11am–6.30pm,
Saturday 10am–2pm.
Fine Italian wines.

Hardy
Warnemünder Straße 15, Wilmersdorf.
Rare wines and brandies.

Nöthlings Weingeschäft
Schloßstraße 28, Steglitz.
Champagnes and fine wines from local vintages to the House of Rothschild.

La cave de Bacchus
Westfälische Straße 33, Wilmersdorf.
Specialist in French wines.

El Campo
Nauheimer Straße 44, Wilmersdorf.
Spanish wines.

Hairdressers

Udo Walz
Kurfürstendamm 200, Wilmersdorf.
Tel: 8827457.
The Berlin hairdresser for VIPs.

Norbert & Theo
Sybelstraße 68, Charlottenburg.
Tel: 8836788.
Quality cuts in elegant surroundings.

Tristan
Isoldestraße 10, Schöneberg.
Tel: 8516010.
A long-time favourite among well-coiffed Berlin women.

Jasons Hair-Power
Leibnizstraße 102, Charlottenburg.
Tel: 3419085.
Extravagant scissoring done here.

Struwwelpeter
Holtzendorffstraße 13, Charlottenburg.
Tel: 3242017.
From dreadlocks to hair extension.

Eating Out

Berlin can hardly be called a culinary mecca but there are indigenous specialities worth trying. These include the proverbial *eisbein* (pigs' knuckles) with sauerkraut and *erbspürree* (mashed peas), and fried herring with potato salad. Another speciality, and a must at Christmas, is goose. Out of season, a *goldbroiler*, or humble roast chicken, will do.

In addition, you will find the ubiquitous *schmalzstullen* (dripping sandwiches), *buletten* (fried meatballs), *senfgurken* (gherkins pickled with mustard seed), *rollmöpse* and *soleier* (pickled eggs) – the staples of any well-stocked Berlin corner pub. Additional treats for the sweet-toothed are *kartoffelpuffer mit apfelmus* (potato pancakes with apple sauce) and *rote grütze mit sahne* (red fruit jelly with whipped cream). It goes without saying that calorific creations such as these must be washed down with plenty of beer and, above all, a decent *klarer* (a shot of 'clear' schnapps). If you conclude that all these fatty staples are mere excuses for Berliners to overindulge in alcohol, you are right. Anyone who wants to make it through the long Berlin nights comes to appreciate the city's heavy cuisine, or, at the very least, that essential morning-after pill: a fat *rollmops*.

The Berliner's favourite food, however, is the *currywurst*. After all, the sausage was invented here, and there is hardly a corner in town without the ubiquitous *wurstbude*. And if not a sausage stand, then a *döner* (kebab) stand. The main thing is that food here be fast and solid – as if the next seige or famine were right around the corner. And let no-one claim that you can get *currywurst* or a *döner* in any other city besides Berlin, where advocates of one fast-food stand or another have fanatical followings. Food is definitely not a laughing matter amongst Berliners.

But aside from tried and tested belly-fillers, there is also fine cuisine of more distinguished provenance here, and plenty of restaurants offering specialities from the four corners of the earth – in other words, something for every Berliner's taste. Since Berlin has thousands of eating establishments, the following selection cannot help but be brief and subjective. In some of these restaurants the cooking is not always first class; it may well be the atmosphere that makes the place worth visiting. So dig in and enjoy! Or, as Berliners say, *Ran an die Buletten!*

Refined Cuisine

Frühsammers Restaurant an der Rehwiese
Matterhornstraße 101, Nikolassee.
Tel: 8032720.
Daily 7–11pm,
Sunday also noon–2pm.
Enchanting dishes celebrated in the most elegant surroundings.

Ponte Vecchio
Spielhagenstraße 3, Charlottenburg.
Tel: 3421999
Daily except Tuesday 6.30–11pm.
No extravagance in the décor, the focus is firmly on first-class food from Northern Italy.

Rockendorfs Restaurant
Düsterhauptstraße 1, Reinickendorf.
Tel: 4023099.
Daily except Sunday and Monday, noon–2pm, 7pm–midnight.
The refined palate pleasers put together by the chef here have been among the finest in town for a decade.

Silhouette
In the Grand Hotel,
Friedrichstraße 158-162, Mitte.
Tel: 2092400.
Daily 11.30am–4pm, 7pm–3am.
Even in Honecker's days the staff here demonstrated that big-city cooks are capable of more than *wienerschnitzel* with starchy fillers on the side. Supply problems were unheard of for his prestige project.

Old Berlin Cuisine

Hardtke
Meinekestraße 27, Wilmersdorf.
Tel: 8819827.
Daily 9am–1am.
Large restaurant which does its own butchering. Ask for a *schnapps* with the *schlachtplatte.*

Max und Moritz
Oranienstraße 162, Kreuzberg.
Tel: 6141045.
Daily 6pm–1.30am.
Pub dating back to the turn of the century. Large portions and Kreuzberg locals digging in with gusto.

Zillemarkt
Bleibtreustraße 48a, Charlottenburg.
Tel: 8814070.
Daily 8pm–2am.
Summer house-style garden setting. Popular for *rollmops* and *bulette*, used as hangover cures, and for those who just want to keep on going.

Zur letzten Instanz
Waisenstr. 14-16, Mitte.
Tel: 2125528.
Monday 3pm–midnight,
Tuesday–Saturday 11am–midnight,
Sunday 11am–4pm.
The oldest pub in Berlin, this place dates back to the 17th century and is usually packed – which merely adds to the atmosphere.

Chinese

Pamela
Rotherstraße 27, Friedrichshain.
Tel: 5892871.
Daily 4pm–midnight.
The best Chinese restaurants are in the east. The 'Soup of Four Things' here is liquid poetry!

Ming's Garden
Tauentzienstraße 16, Schöneberg.
Tel: 2118728.
Daily noon–midnight.
Cantonese, Peking and Shanghai-style cuisine in an elegant setting.

Eastern European

Kalinka
Am Festungsgraben 1, Mitte.
Tel: 2001227.
Monday–Friday 11am–midnight.
Russian restaurant, hidden away, offering good, solid and tasty food.

Moskau
Karl-Marx-Allee 34, Mitte.
Tel: 2792869.
Daily 11am–midnight.
Very good cooking for those who like strong flavours. The bar is a charming place for downing a drink or two.

Polonaise
Ferdinandstraße 33, Steglitz.
Tel: 7721500.
Daily noon–1am.
Unlike restaurants in Poland, where there are supply problems, here you can taste true Polish cuisine. Calorie-counters should give this a miss.

Schwejk
Ansbacher Straße 4, Schöneberg.
Tel: 2137892.
Daily from 6pm on.
Bohemian cuisine and fresh beer in the proper atmosphere.

French

Abricot
Hasenheide 48, Kreuzberg.
Tel: 6931150.
Wednesday–Monday 6pm–1am.
Near Südstern. A younger crowd also comes here to treat themselves to the delights of French culinary art.

Florian
Grolmannstraße 52, Charlottenburg.
Tel: 3139184.
Daily 6pm–3am.
The menu is not strictly French, but that does not matter. This is where the film world gathers, as well as all the folks keen on star spotting.

Paris Bar
Kantstraße 152, Charlottenburg.
Tel: 31380.
Monday–Saturday noon–1am.
Bistro restaurant where bohemians meet – along with many a merry group spun off from the film festival.

Greek

Fofi's Estatorio
Fasanenstraße 70, Wilmersdorf.
Tel: 8818785.
Daily 7pm on.
Greek *haute cuisine*.

TA PANTA REI
Düsseldorfer Straße 75, Wilmersdorf.
Tel: 877346.
Daily 5pm–1am.
Cosy surroundings, with unpretentious and refined cuisine.

TERZO MONDO
Grolmannstraße 28, Charlottenburg.
Tel: 8815261.
Daily 6pm–2am.
The food is nothing special, but this is the traditional watering hole of the Old Left, as well as a magnet for *Lindenstraße* (a German TV series) addicts, who come just to take a look at Kostas, the owner.

Italian

BAR CENTRALE
Yorckstraße 82, Kreuzberg.
Tel: 7862989
Daily 5pm–3am.
Bar and restaurant with relaxed atmosphere. Either spend the evening with a beer or enjoy the fine food.

BORBONE
Windscheidstraße 14, Charlottenburg.
Tel: 3238305.
Daily noon–midnight.
Rustic interior, but with the choicest dishes and very charming waiters.

DON CAMILLO
Schloßstraße 7, Charlottenburg.
Tel: 3223572.
Thursday–Tuesday noon–3pm, 6–11.30pm.
A top-quality *ristorante*.

FIORETTO
Oberspreestraße 176, Köpenick.
Tel: 6572605.
Tuesday–Saturday 6–12pm, Sunday 11.30am–11pm.
A surprise in the east: fine Italian cooking which left many speechless long before the fall of the wall.

HOSTARIA DEL MONTE CROCE
Mittenwalder Straße 6, Kreuzberg.
Tel: 6943968.
Daily except Sunday 7.30pm on.
Tiny restaurant, located in a courtyard. Food is served unordered in large quantities. Empty bottles are cleared and replaced with full ones.

SAVOIA
Windscheidstraße 31, Charlottenburg.
Tel: 3241870.
Daily noon–3pm, 6pm–midnight.
Elegance and outstanding cuisine.

Japanese

KYOTO
Wilmersdorfer Straße 94, Charlottenburg. Tel: 8832733.
Daily noon–2pm, 6pm–midnight.
Excellent and popular sushi bar.

SAPPORO-KAN
Schlüterstraße 52, Charlottenburg.
Tel: 8812973.
Daily noon–2pm, 6pm–midnight, Sunday from 6pm–midnight.
Popular with Japanese families.

UDAGAWA
Feuerbachstraße 24, Steglitz.
Tel: 7922373.
Wednesday–Monday 11.30am–2.30pm, 5.30–11.30pm.
Simple but perfect Japanese cuisine.

Turkish

Bagdad
Schlesische Straße 2, Kreuzberg.
Tel: 6126962.
Daily 11am–midnight.
An oasis of Oriental hospitality situated deep in the heart of lively Kreuzberg. The Kreuzberg in-crowd enjoys sitting around in the kitsch-romantic garden here.

Hitit
Danckelmannstraße/Ecke Knobelsdorffstraße, Charlottenburg.
Tel: 3224557.
Daily 6pm–1am.
Refined Turkish cuisine – with elegantly stylized ambience.

Öz Samsun
Karl-Marx-Straße 16-18, Neukölln.
Tel: 6224764.
Daily noon–3pm.
Simple and elegant with fine cuisine. Belly-dancing with piano accompaniment at weekends draws Berliners returning from excursions.

Vegetarian

Café Tiago
Knesebeckstraße 15, Charlottenburg.
Tel: 3129042.
Monday–Saturday 8–2am,
Sunday 10–2am.
Wonderful small dishes in a former Sanyasin café. This is the place where the young people from Savignyplatz go for breakfast.

Hakuin
Martin-Luther-Straße 3, Schöneberg.
Tel: 242027.
Wednesday–Tuesday 6–11.30pm, Saturday and Sunday noon–3pm.
Zen meditation along with excellent food – in an atmosphere which, through its very purity and restraint, is spiritually satisfying

Thürnagel
Gneisenaustraße 57, Kreuzberg.
Tel: 6914800.
Daily 6pm–midnight.
Wholefoods, but without any of the grim seriousness and rigorous ideology which sometimes accompanies wholefood cooking. This is an elegant organic restaurant.

Midnight Nibbles

Café Tiago
Knesebeckstraße 15, Charlottenburg.
Tel: 3129042.
Sunday–Thursday 11–4am,
Friday and Saturday 11–5am.
Located right next to the Far Out disco. Night owls stop off here for one last *gyros*.

Ca va
Pariser Straße 56, Wilmersdorf.
Tel: 8833674.
Daily 5pm–6am.
Southern German and vegetarian food in a simple atmosphere.

Leibniz-Klause
Leibnizstraße 46, Charlottenburg,.
Tel: 3237068.
Daily 11.30–7am.
Eisbein in the first light of dawn? Well, it certainly is an experience.

Schöneberger Weltlaterne
Motzstraße 61, Schöneberg.
Tel: 2116247.
Daily 11–3am.
Good solid food – roast pork at midnight, for example – as the basis for another round of partying or the re-energising last stop of the evening.

Uhlwig
Uhlandstraße 49, Wilmersdorf.
Tel: 8821361.
Daily noon–4am.
Feel like *couscous* at 3am? Then this is the place to go!

Bars and Pubs

CUT
Knesebeckstraße 16, Charlottenburg.
Tel: 3133511. Daily 10pm–6am.
Black marble and mirrors, over 300 cocktails and many a familiar face from the theatre scene.

GEIER
Prenzlauer Promenade 3, Weißensee.
Tel: 3563517.
Random opening times; in the evening until the last guest goes.
Currently the wildest joint in Berlin, the place where the in-crowd from east and the west get together.

MADONNA
Wiener Straße 22, Kreuzberg.
Tel: 6116943.
Daily from 11am until the last guest leaves.
This venue is jam–packed, the music blaring. The guests range from Kreuzberg locals to hedonistic bank clerks! It's the best introduction to wild Kreuzberg nights.

MÖWE
Hermann-Matern-Straße 18, Mitte.
Tel: 2805121.
Tuesday–Saturday noon–5am.
This elegant plush interior is where established artists of the former GDR used to meet. The well-to-do and celebrities are still most welcome.

ZUR WEIßEN MAUS
Ludwigkirchplatz 12, Wilmersdorf.
Tel: 8822264. Daily 9pm–5am.
Elegant bohemians meet here in 1920s-style surroundings. The door check, however, is rigorous.

For Women or Men Only

ANDREAS' KNEIPE
Ansbacher Straße 29, Schöneberg.
Tel: 243257.
Daily 11–4am.
A touch of flannel, a hint of grey hair, but men are said to enjoy themselves here.

EXTRA DRY
Mommsenstraße 34, Charlottenburg.
Tel: 3246068.
Tuesday–Thursday noon–11pm.
Café/restaurant for women who don't drink alcohol; the atmosphere is so pleasant, you may not want to leave.

Knast
Fuggerstraße 34, Schöneberg.
Tel: 2411026.
Daily 9pm–5am.
Men in leather. To each his/her own.

Lipstick
Richard-Wagner-Platz 5, Charlottenburg.
Tel: 3428126.
Daily 10pm–5am.
Cocktail bar for lively women. On Monday, additional admission for men seeking men.

Pour Elle
Kalkreuthstraße 10, Schöneberg.
Tel: 245733.
Tuesday–Sunday 9pm–5am.
Here you will find a refined bar and discothèque for ladies who can do very well without men, thank you.

SchwuZ
Hasenheide 54, Kreuzberg.
Tel: 6941077.
Café, Friday 9pm–2am; Disco, Saturday 10pm on.
This is a gay centre and gay 'community' meeting place.

Nightclubs

Blue Note
Coubièrestraße 13, Schöneberg.
Tel: 247248.
Tuesday–Sunday 10pm–5am.
This club features an intimate disco with cool music. It is even possible to carry on a conversation here, and the bouncer is very sweet.

Dschungel
Nürnberger Straße 53, Schöneberg.
Tel: 246698.
Tuesday–Sunday 10pm–3am.
This is the ultimate in-crowd disco. Whoever passes the door check can rest assured of his/her social prospects for the rest of the evening: if you get in, you've arrived. Inside it is chock-a-block and the dance floor is miniscule. But seeing and being seen is the name of the game here.

Cha Cha
NürnbergerStraße50, Schöneberg.
Tel: 2142976.
Tuesday–Sunday 11pm–6am.
The good news is that those who are turned away at Dschungel can try here. The bad news is that it is not easy to get into the Cha Cha either.

Far Out
Kurfürstendamm 156, Wilmersdorf.
Tel: 3200723.
Tuesday–Sunday 10pm–6am.
Here at last, a place where everyone is allowed in. The music has a good danceable beat and the people are very friendly.

Yucca-Bar
Neumannstraße 136, Pankow.
Tel: 4728880.
Monday–Saturday 8pm–2am.
Men who look loaded, and women looking for them, frequent this venue: elegant ambience in the VIP neighbourhood of the former SED.

Live Music

QUASIMODO
Kantstraße 12a, Charlottenburg.
Tel: 3128086.
Rock, jazz and blues.

LOHMEYERS
Eosanderstraße 24, Charlottenburg.
Tel: 3429660.
Swing and jazz.

FLÖZ
Nassauische Straße 37, Wilmersdorf.
Tel: 8611000.
Cabaret with jazz performances.

FRANZ-CLUB
Schönhauser Allee 36-39,
Prenzlauer Berg.
Tel: 4485567.
Wonderful blues, rock and jazz says a Prenzelberger.

Calendar of Special Events

Berlin is really one year-long round of festivities. The season begins with the spring festival on Lützowplatz, and the fair in the Kultur Park in Treptow – which lasts practically the whole year round – followed by the blossom celebrations (*Baumblüte*) in Britz and Werder. The summer calendar is full of events: the *Spandauer Havelfest* and the *Festwochen* ('Festive Weeks') in Köpenick and Steglitz; the various people's festivals (*Volksfeste*) celebrating bilateral 'friendship' (German-American, German-French, German-Soviet); the *Turmstraßenfest;* the *Kreuzberger Festliche Tage* and the *Oktoberfest* (any resemblance to Munich's beer festival is coincidental). Finally, there are the Christmas markets on Alexanderplatz and Breitscheidplatz. In other words, there is always a fair going on somewhere. There are almost as many festivals and (trade) fairs. For the exact dates, which vary slightly from year to year, contact the Berliner Festspiel (Tel: 25489-0).

JANUARY–FEBRUARY

Internationale Grüne Woche (International Green Week). This huge nosh-up, with mountains of fresh food from all over the world, gives the food industry and agricultural trade a chance to show off their wares. Masses throng through the Messehallen am Funkturm (the convention centre located at the broadcasting tower), tasting thousands of titbits, sipping beverage samples, complaining about inflated prices and studying the life of pigs, only – after tasting all these exotic foods – to return to their familiar *currywurst*.

MID-FEBRUARY

Internationale Filmfestspiele (International Film Festival). A festival of cinematic superlatives or, at least, the most important film festival after those at Cannes and Venice. Getting tickets is not as hard as you might think. There are fewer movie stars these days, as the glory of the event's early years has worn off. Nevertheless, the festival is an opportunity to see movies which never find a distributor, and dark horses here have often turned out to be big box office hits.

MARCH

Internationale Tourismus-Börse (International Tourism Convention). The annual venue for people in the travel industry, as well as members of the general public interested in information about nearby sights and faraway places. Often, a visit here serves as a substitute for the journey itself, as there is plenty of stimulation for the armchair traveller.

APRIL

Berliner Kunsttage (Berlin Art Days). The Berlin art scene advertises itself here through exhibitions, studio presentations and various other events. **Freie Berliner Kunstausstellung**, or FBK (Free Berlin Art Exhibition). This is the ultimate art show, giving anyone painting pictures or creating sculpture a chance to present their work to an interested public. Many artists have been discovered here.

MAY–JUNE

Theatertreffen (Theatre Summit). A presentation of top German theatre productions selected by a professional jury, the performances and other accompanying events at the 'summit' are a sheer delight for theatre-lovers.

JULY

Jazz in July. Small, privately organised annual jazz club festival.

AUGUST–SEPTEMBER

Funkausstellung (Broadcasting Exhibition). Every odd-numbered year television and radio celebrate their achievements: entertainment is growing increasingly shallow, the technical innovations more superfluous.

SEPTEMBER–OCTOBER

Berliner Festwochen (Berlin Cultural Festival). International artists, orchestras and theatre groups present a potpourri of their creative work at venues throughout the city.

OCTOBER–NOVEMBER

Jazz-Fest Berlin. This renowned jazz festival features established stars and, occasionally, undiscovered talent.

Berlin has the year-round appeal of one of the most exciting cities in the world: its attractions are just as splendid no matter what the season. People do not come to Berlin as a summer resort, but are drawn here by its history and culture. Nevertheless, summer is without question the prettiest time of year – when even the tenement districts exude a certain charm. And, above all, the summer weather also turns the otherwise rather gruff and hectic Berliners into friendly, good-natured creatures.

On beautiful summer days half of Berlin flocks to the city's various green oases. The parks are full of life and there is one street or district festival after another. The city begins to take on an almost Mediterranean ambience, as pubs and restaurants move tables and chairs out onto the pavement on the mild summer nights. It is no coincidence that most Berliners choose the dismal, cold season for their own holidays in more temperate regions. After all, Berlin in the summertime has everything one needs for holidays in 'Balconia'. Guests in town for a week may want to pack smart clothes (for elegant dining and dancing) as well as jeans (for nights in Kreuzberg) and swimwear (for Wannsee Beach).

Tourist Information

For hotel reservations, as well as general tourist information, please contact the Fremdenverkehrsbüro (Tourist Information Bureau) in the Europa-Center, Berlin 30, Budapester Straße entrance; Tel: 2123-4 or 26260-31/33; daily 7.30am–10.30pm. There is an additional information centre at Hardenbergstraße 20 in Charlottenburg (Berlin 12); Tel: 310040; open Monday–Friday 8am–7pm and Saturday 8am–4pm.

GETTING THERE

By Car

The days when Berlin had a reputation as the most driver-friendly city in Germany are ancient history. The number of accidents on the motorways into Berlin are increasing, traffic jams are the order of the day and, in peak traffic at weekends and holidays, it seems as if a bicycle would be a faster way to get from Hanover to Berlin than a car. All environmental qualms aside, for the sake of your physical and mental health, it is recommended that you leave your car at home.

Within the city itself, driving is one of the best ways to ruin your stay in Berlin. Even on the generously laid out Ringstraße (ring road) stop-and-go-traffic is the rule. For the dubious pleasure of perpetual congestion, try any one of the main arteries. And rush-hour driving – especially if you are not yet used to the Berliner's aggressive driving style – is a good way to test the limits of your ability to handle stress. However, this is one experience you can probably do without. I will spare you descriptions of the agonizing experience of parking. Anyone who manages to find a space free of charge leaves his car there permanently and uses the excellent public transportation system complete with U- and S-Bahn (Underground) trains, as well as buses and trams serving practically every corner of the city – departing at regular and convenient intervals.

There are taxis in every large square in town, and they also prowl the main thoroughfares: even late at night you should be able to flag one down. Hotels, restaurants and pubs will also call a cab for you upon request.

The numbers of the largest radio taxi firms are: West Berlin: 240024/6902/261026/240202. East Berlin: 3366/3644.

By Train

Granted, the old-fashioned Reichsbahn railroad system in Berlin is not up to West German standards. The expansion and upgrading campaign has been assigned top priority, however, so within a few years the train will be the most pleasant means of travel to and from Berlin. To date, there is only one Inter-city service to Berlin: the one from Hamburg. On the other hand, the frequency of departures has been increased and – with the elimination of the elaborate border checks – travel time has been reduced. From Hanover there are also Interregro-class trains. In Berlin you can get off at one of three stations. Most people disembark at the Bahnhof Zoologischer Garten which is right in the middle of the western city. Recent renovation has greatly improved its appearance. Bahnhof Friedrichstraße, located in Berlin-Mitte, the historic heart of Berlin, is the destination of choice for people who either live in the vicinity or have reservations in one of the excellent hotels nearby. The Hauptbahnhof Friedrichshain is of interest mainly for travellers continuing to Eastern Europe. This is where the respective connecting trains depart.

Information:
Bahnhof Zoo: Tel: 19419 or 31102111.
Bahnhof Friedrichstraße: Tel: 49534 or 49541.

By Air

Although Berlin already has four airports, an additional one is being planned outside the city. One of the airports, Gatow, is used exclusively by the British Allied Air Force. Some domestic airlines fly into Flughafen Tempelhof. Schönefeld, rather more functional than pleasant, largely serves the eastern hemisphere. Tegel, on the other hand, is the international airport with flights to and from points all over the world. Like Tempelhof, however, it is right in the middle of the city, so take-offs and landings are

prohibited at night.
Information:
Flughafen Tegel: Tel: 41011.
Flughafen Schönefeld: Tel: 6720.
Flughafen Tempelhof: Tel: 69091.

MONEY MATTERS

There are automatic cash points throughout the city – increasingly even in East Berlin. The better hotels are also willing to cash cheques. Banking hours are from 9am–3.30pm, and some banks have a late service when they stay open until 6pm.

There is additional after-hours banking at: Bahnhof Zoo (train station), Monday–Saturday 8am–9pm, Sunday 10am–6pm and Flughafen Tegel (airport), daily 6.30am–9pm.

TOPOGRAPHY

Geography

Berlin is the largest city in Germany both in terms of size and population. Located at a latitude of 52.31 North and longitude of 13.24 East, it covers 883km² (340 square miles) of sandy Brandenburg Marches terrain. The city has a total circumference of 229km (143 miles). In an east-west direction it reaches a maximum width of 45km (28 miles) and in a north-south direction, 38km (24 miles).

Of Berlin's present population of 3.4 million, 280,000 are foreigners. By the year 2000 experts expect Berlin to swell to a population of 5 million, while pessimists expect a figure closer to 10 million.

Living in a city at an average elevation of 34m (110ft) above sea level in the heart of the northern German lowlands, Berliners enjoy calling their few hills mountains. The highest natural elevation are the Müggelberge near Köpenick, rising to a height of 115m (375ft). Many of the *berge*, though – such as the Teufelsberg, or 'Devil's Mountain', in Grunewald – are actually heaped-up mounds of rubble dating from World War II.

For the best panoramic views of the city, try either the restaurant in the television tower, the Fernsehturm, or the observation platform on top of the Europa-Center next to the Gedächtniskirche.

Districts

It was not until the incorporation of numerous surrounding communities, villages and cities in 1920 that Berlin became the metropolis it is today. Smaller communities merged into administrative districts named after the largest community. The following list of districts, along with the respective integrated villages, should help you to find your way around:

West Berlin
Reinickendorf: Frohnau, Heiligensee, Konradshöhe, Tegel, Hermsdorf, Waidmannslust, Lübars, Wittenau
Wedding
Spandau: Staaken, Haselhorst, Siemensstadt, Gatow, Kladow
Tiergarten
Charlottenburg
Wilmersdorf: Grunewald, Schmargendorf
Schöneberg: Friedenau

Kreuzberg
Zehlendorf: Wannsee, Nikolassee, Dahlem
Steglitz: Lichterfelde, Lankwitz
Tempelhof: Mariendorf, Marienfelde, Lichtenrade
Neukölln: Britz, Buckow, Rudow

Ost-Berlin (East Berlin)
Pankow: Buch, Blankenfelde, Buchholz, Rosenthal, Niederschönhausen
Weißensee: Karow, Blankenburg, Heinersdorf, Malchow
Hohenschönhausen: Wartenberg, Falkenberg
Prenzlauer Berg
Mitte
Friedrichshain
Lichtenberg: Friedrichsfelde, Karlshorst
Marzahn: Biesdorf
Hellersdorf: Kaulsdorf, Mahlsdorf
Treptow: Baumschulenweg, Niederschöneweide, Johannisthal, Adlershof, Altglienicke, Bohnsdorf
Köpenick: Oberschöneweide, Friedrichshagen, Rahnsdorf, Müggelheim, Grünau, Schmöckwitz

Climate and Clothing

The climate in Berlin is moderate. Summer can be very hot and quite unpleasant. The winters are generally mild, but there are also harsh cold spells. Whenever there is thermal inversion – especially in the winter, when the smog from domestic heating and industrial chimneys is particularly bad – it is hard to imagine that Berlin is famous for its air. Warm clothing is a good idea even in summer, since it occasionally gets quite cool at night.

There are hardly any social dress requirements. Certain bars or discothèques have door checks, but even then, the emphasis is more on originality and personal flair than on conventional dress requirements. Jeans are fine for the theatre, the casino (the only requirement being ties for men), or even the opera. Casualness is an important part of the Berlin lifestyle.

Language and People

Berliners are rough diamonds and from a distance they can seem quite brusque. But if there is one thing they appreciate it is directness, and if you ask them politely but firmly for information, they can become downright pleasant. Older people – if you happen upon one of the more obliging species, that is, since senior Berliners can be particularly grumpy – will not only provide the information requested but also, gladly and unasked, share their wealth of personal experience.

Certain segments of the city's population display a marked hostility towards clearly-defined groups of foreigners such as Third World refugees or immigrant workers, and so some Berliners are keen on making anyone who looks too 'foreign' feel unwelcome. Typically, as a visitor, you will find yourself overwhelmed by offers of assistance or plied with more information than you really need – provided you make the first move. Berliners love to 'gab', preferably about themselves, especially at bus stops or during Underground rides; if you have the time and are a good listener, you may hear a story or two, revealing more about the city and its people than many a history book.

Younger people display more curt manners. They may divulge a friendly and almost intimate answer to your question one moment and then abruptly take their leave the next. Chance meetings which lead to conversation usually end with the classic phrase: 'Let's phone one another.' This is a suggestion rarely acted upon. The most cordial contacts take place in pubs – provided you do not encroach on a stranger's table. At the bar though, you may quickly become somebody's best friend for a couple of hours. Here, too, you should bear in mind that everything is acted out in the 'here and now' and usually remains without consequence.

In terms of language, Berlin is one great big Tower of Babel. The city's dialect is the result of a variety of cultural influences. The vocabulary is full of Huguenot and Yiddish, with traces of Swabian and Saxon in the prevailing accent. Local jargon includes Turkish (nobody says *kebab* when they mean *döner*), Italian (as a casual word of farewell, *ciao*! is strong competition for the German *tschüss*!) and Eastern European (*datsche* for a weekend cottage). Nearly everyone speaks English – usually somewhat broken but more than adequate for most purposes.

SIGHTSEEING

Packing a map is recommended for getting around in Berlin. It is no wonder that even natives cannot explain how to find everything. After all, the city is huge, and East and West Berliners are only now beginning to rediscover the respective other halves of their city. You will find good guides and maps in any bookshop or department store. The best overall map of Greater Berlin is the *RV Großraum-Stadtatlas, Berlin*. It is too large, however, to carry around on walking tours. Although they only cover the inner city area, the Falk-Verlag tourist maps are more practical.

An individual walking tour of the city is always more fun than an organised sightseeing excursion, but the latter is quicker and more comfortable. Not only are there numerous operators offering coach tours, but – in a city criss-crossed with canals, rivers and other waterways – you may

also want to consider one of the various sightseeing boats as a charming way to see the city. For individualists, I recommend a tram or bus ride. A trip on one of the two lines crossing practically the entire city allows passengers to gain a thorough impression of everyday life on the streets of Berlin.

From its point of departure, Am Kupfergraben near the Museumsinsel, Tram 70 crosses the Scheunenviertel and the Prenzlauer Berg, then passes through Weißensee to the turn-around in Hohenschönhausen. Bus 29 starts at Roseneck in the Grunewald district, travels the entire length of the Kurfürstendamm to Landwehrkanal, passes the former Checkpoint Charlie and follows Oranienstraße through Kreuzberg before reaching Hermannplatz in Neukölln.

Tour Boat Lines

Reederei Bruno Winkler
Levetzowstraße 16,
Tel: 39170-10/70.

Reederei Heinz Riedel
Planufer 78,
Tel: 6913782/6934646.

Stern-und Kreisschiffahrt
Sachtlebenstraße 60,
Tel: 8031055/8038750.

Spreefahrt
Boat journeys on the River Spree.

Horst Duggen,
Regensburger Straße 8, Tel: 3944954.

Weiße Flotte ('White Fleet')
Rosa-Luxemburg-Straße 2,
Tel: 27123-27/28.

Guided City Tours

Berliner Bären-Stadtrundfahrten
Rankestraße 35, Tel: 2134077.

Berolina-Stadtrundfahrten
Kurfürstendamm 228, Tel: 8822063.

Holiday Sightseeing Berlin
Fasanenstraße 67, Tel: 88420711.

Severin & Kühn
Kurfürstendamm 216, Tel: 8831115.

Theme-Orientated Guided Tours

Berliner Geschichtwerkstatt (Berlin Historical Workshop)
Goltzstraße 49, Tel: 2154450.

Kultur Kontor ('Cultural Office')
Savignyplatz 9–10, Tel: 310888.

Stattreisen Berlin eV (Alternative Tours)
Stephanstraße 24, Tel: 3953078.

Car Rental (with driver)

Brocke
Straße 366, Tel: 4313010.
Auto chauffeur service.

Minibus Service
Zietenstraße 1, Tel: 2611456.

Oldtimer-Taxi Berlin
Reiner Dieckert,
Dürerstraße 28c, Tel: 8338867.

Royalty Rolls Royce
P Andersen,
Alt-Mariendorf 9, Tel: 7055320.

Car Rental (self-drive)

AVIS
Budapester Straße 30, Tel: 2611881.
Tegel Airport, Tel: 4101-3148.

Hertz
Central Reservations, Tel: 01302121.

InterRent
Tegel Airport, Tel: 410133-54/68.
Kurfürstendamm 178–9, Tel: 8818093.

Public Transport (BVG)
Criss-crossed with a network of U- and S-Bahn (Underground) trains and buses – and, in East Berlin, trams –

Berlin is the easiest place in the world to do without a private car. Even at night there is no problem getting around since numerous buses provide all-night service. Two of the most important underground (U-Bahn) lines also run all night (on Friday and Saturday every quarter of an hour): the U9, the north-south train from Wedding to Steglitz; the U1, from Kreuzberg nearly all the way to Spandau. Both lines cross most of the important night bus lines.

Berlin has a non-zoned fare system, which means that tickets are valid for the entire city and for all means of transportation. As of June 1991 the single ticket costs 3DM and is also valid for suburban train (S-Bahn) rides into the surrounding countryside; to Nauen, for example, Wustermark, Potsdam, Schönefeld, Königs Wusterhausen, Fürstenwalde, Strausberg, Bernau or Oranienburg. There are ticket machines at all stations. A ticket is valid for two hours, and you can even double back or zig-zag as long as you do not exceed this time limit.

The U2, cut by the building of the wall, will probably be reconnected by the end of 1992. It will then run from Krumme Lanke (Zehlendorf) via the currently shut-down stations Nollendorfplatz and Bülowstraße to Pankow. The U-Bahn and S-Bahn station Potsdamer Platz will also be re-opened in the next couple of years.

ACCOMMODATION

During the cultural festivals, trade fairs and conferences, hotels are totally booked up. The flood of tourists has increased since the opening of the wall. Unless you have alternative accommodation, a spur-of-the-moment trip to Berlin can be marred by an unpleasant or futile search for a hotel room. Reservations made several weeks in advance are definitely recommended.

Luxury Hotels

Bristol Hotel Kempinski
Kurfürstendamm 27. Tel: 88434-0.
Single 380–430, double 430–480DM.
The epitome of traditional luxury.

Grand Hotel
Friedrichstraße 158–164, Mitte.
Tel: 20923253/4.
Single 380, double 480DM.
By far the most beautiful hotel in town in immaculate neo-Wilhelminian style.

Grand Hotel Esplanade
Lützowufer 15. Tel: 261011.
Single 300, double 350DM.
The modern, polished design emphasises functional luxury.

Inter-Continental
Budapester Straße 2. Tel: 2602-0.
Single 345, double 395DM.
The largest hotel in town. Famous for its luxury.

Palast Hotel
Karl-Liebknecht-Straße 5, Mitte.
Tel: 2412384.
Single 250–320, double 340–390DM.
Ex-GDR luxury; a bit conventional but with all the trimmings.

First-Class Hotels

Art Hotel Sorat
Joachimstaler Straße 28–29.
Tel: 8844470.
Single 195, double 235DM.
Art and accommodation: the Wolf Vostell designer furniture and sculptures make each room a unique experience.

Avantgarde
Kurfürstendamm 15. Tel: 8826466.
Singles 210, doubles 320DM.
Neo-Baroque house with huge rooms decorated with stucco mouldings.

ARTEMISIA
Brandenburgische Straße 18.
Tel: 876373.
Single 100-125, double 139-200DM.
Tiny, attractively decorated hotel reserved exclusively for women.

DOM HOTEL
Mohrenstraße 30, Mitte. Tel: 2098-0.
Single 215–350, double 340–420DM.
Fine modern hotel overlooking the most beautiful square in the city: the Platz der Akademie.

MONDIAL
Kurfürstendamm 47. Tel: 884110.
Single 170–300, double 220–400DM.
Spacious rooms. The entire hotel is designed for use by the handicapped.

RESIDENZ
Meinekestraße 9. Tel: 88443-0.
Single 180, double 240DM.
Art nouveau décor.

RIEHMERS HOFGARTEN
Yorckstraße 83. Tel: 781011.
Single 146, double 186DM.
Located in one of the most beautiful residential complexes in Berlin.

SAVOY
Fasanenstraße 9–10. Tel: 31103-0.
Single 245, double 400DM.
Comfortable and modern, in the centre.

SCHWEIZERHOF
Budapester Straße 21–31. Tel: 2696-0.
Single 380, double 430DM.
Tasteful and comfortable.

SEEHOF
Lietzensee Ufer 11. Tel: 32002-0.
Single 175-235, double 280DM.
Idyllic lakeside location, a 2-minute walk from the ICC Conference Centre.

STEIGENBERGER
Los-Angeles-Platz 1. Tel: 2108-0.
Single 370, double 450DM.
Chain hotel with ready-made luxury.

Hotels and Pensions

ALPINA
Trabener Straße 3. Tel: 8916090.
Single from 80DM, double from 130DM.
Small villa with a garden near the Grunewald S-Bahn station.

KREUZBERG
Großbeerenstraße 64. Tel: 2511362.
Single from 30DM, double from 50DM.
For young, undemanding guests.

SAVOY
Meinekestraße 4. Tel: 8813700.
Single from 90DM, double from 120DM.
Small but nice.

TERMINUS
Fasanenstraße 48. Tel: 8814909.
Single from 30DM, double from 35DM.
Neither plush nor dingy.

TRANSIT
Hagelberger Straße 53–54,
Tel: 7855051.
Single from 45DM, double from 70DM.
Charming hotel for young people who care more for atmosphere than luxury.

Camping

In West Berlin, contact:
DEUTSCHER CAMPING-CLUB
Geisbergstraße 11, Tel: 6571413.
In East Berlin:
BEZIRKSAMT KÖPENICK
Am Katzengraben 20, Tel: 6571413.

Youth Accommodation

JUGENDHERBERGE BAYERNALLEE (YOUTH HOSTEL)
Bayernallee 36. Tel: 3053055.

JUGENDGÄSTEHAUS AM WANNSEE (YOUTH GUEST HOUSE)
Badeweg 1. Tel: 8032034.

JUGENDGÄSTEHAUS BERLIN (YOUTH GUEST HOUSE)
Kluckstraße 3. Tel: 26110-97–8.

JUGENDGÄSTEHAUS AM ZOO (YOUTH GUEST HOUSE)
Hardenbergstraße 9a. Tel: 3129410.

JUGENDTOURISTENHOTEL (YOUTH TOURIST HOTEL)
Franz-Mett-Straße 7, Tel: 5100114.

Private Accommodation ('Mitwohnzentralen')

MITWOHNZENTRALE KUDAMM-ECK
Kurfürstendamm 227–228.
Tel: 8826694.
Monday–Friday 10am–7pm,
Saturday and Sunday 11am–3pm.

FRAUEN-MITWOHNZENTRALE
Kurfürstendamm 227–228.
Tel: 8826284.
Monday–Friday 10am–7pm,
Saturday and Sunday 11am–3pm.

MITWOHNZENTRALE BERLIN
Wiener Straße 14. Tel: 61820-08–9.
Monday–Friday 10am–7pm,
Saturday and Sunday 11am–3pm.

MITSCHLAFZENTRALE
Reichenberger Straße 54. Tel: 6118001.

AGENTUR WOHNWITZ (LIVE-IN AGENCY)
Immanuelkirchstraße 11,
Prenzlauer Berg.
Tel: 4392494/4376679.
Monday–Friday 11am–8pm,
Saturday and Sunday 11am–2pm.

BUSINESS HOURS

The official business hours are 9am–6.30pm. On Thursday most shops stay open until 8.30pm. In summer many of the shops around the Kurfürstendamm stay open until 9pm on Friday.

Late-night groceries are available in the following underground (U-Bahn) stations: Schloßstraße (until 10pm), Fehrbelliner Platz (until 10.30pm) and Kurfürstendamm (until 11pm).

INFORMATION & EMERGENCIES

Medical emergencies and fire department: 112.
Police emergencies: 110.
Poisoning emergencies: 3935466.
Poisoning emergencies for children: 3023022.
Doctor on call: 310031.
Emergency medical service (East Berlin): 1259.

Emergency chemist (East Berlin): 160.
German Red Cross (DRK) paramedic service: 85005-5.
After-hours chemists: 1141.
Emergency veterinary service: 1141.
Emergency dental service: 1141.
Berliner Aidshilfe (AIDS Line): 19411.
Drug emergency service: 247033.
Women's crisis line: 654242.
Non-medical practitioner on call (Saturday/Sunday): 8919079.
Youth emergency line: 344026.
Children's emergency line: 61006-333.
Central ambulance co-ordination: 19222.
Emergency line and counselling for rape victims: 2512828.
Lawyer on call for emergency criminal matters: 8823728.
Schwule Wut (Gay Assault Victim Line): 2163336.
Samaritans: 11101.
Lankwitz Tierheim (animal shelter): 7721064.

Consulates

GREAT BRITAIN
Uhlandstraße 7, Tel: 2137033.
UNITED STATES OF AMERICA
Clayallee 170, Tel: 8324087.

Additional Information

ACE auto breakdown service: 19216.
ADAC city auto breakdown service: 19211.
AVD auto breakdown service: 240091.
Motor vehicle assistance (East Berlin): 166.
BVG (public transportation), schedule information: 2165088.
BVG customer service bureau: 3339833.
Train information (west): 19419.
Scheduled departure times: 11531.
Scheduled arrival times: 11532.
Train information (east):
Domestic travel: 49531.
Foreign travel: 49541.
Environmental hotline: 2586-2525.

Lost and Found

West Berlin:
BVG (PUBLIC TRANSPORT) FUNDBÜRO,
Potsdamer Straße 184, Tel: 2161413.
Monday/Tuesday/Thursday 9am–3pm,
Wednesday 9am–6pm,
Friday 9am– 2pm.
FUNDBÜRO DER POLIZEI
(POLICE LOST AND FOUND)
Templehofer Damm 3, Tel: 699-0.
East Berlin:
Wilhelm-Pieck-Straße 164,
Tel: 2829403.
Monday/Wednesday–Friday 9am–4pm,
Tuesday 9am–7pm.
REICHSBAHN (ALSO S-BAHN) FUNDBÜRO
Marx-Engels-Platz S-Bahn station,
Tel: 4921671.
Monday/Thursday/Friday 10am–4pm,
Tuesday 10am -6pm,
Wednesday 10am–5pm.

MEDIA & COMMUNICATION

Newspapers

Since the war, the newspaper market has been dominated by one publishing house: Springer-Verlag. This company's flagship publications are *Bild*, *BZ* and *Morgenpost* – the latter a serious but ultra-conservative periodical.

Although rather fussy and dry, the 'old maid' among the liberal daily newspapers, the *Tagesspiegel* makes a serious effort to avoid too strong a bias in its reporting, but since the opening of the wall it is having a hard time maintaining its leading position. It now has a serious competitor in the form of the *Berliner Zeitung* – a formerly communist East Berlin daily revived by a transfusion of West German journalists. Once very much a leftist underground newspaper, *taz* is now Berlin's only 'national' newspaper; it has shifted more towards the established Left and has become an essential source of information.

As might be expected, major changes are taking place in the Berlin press landscape. East Berlin newspapers, like the former Communist Party organ *Neues Deutschland*, are trying to get the hang of the democratic style of news reporting which is something very new to them. Teaching old dogs new tricks is no easy venture though, and most of the newspapers are in danger of folding. Some ambitious papers are already planning new projects – inspired by the memory of the great newspaper town Berlin was during the 1920s, when 160 papers waged a daily battle for readers. That hardly seems applicable, though, in this age of expanding electronic media.

Three interesting publications worth singling out from the broad spectrum of periodicals are the monthly *Constructiv*, a critical journal with a broad base of contributors; the *Weltbühne*, presenting political articles on current affairs; and the music magazine, *Motiv*.

The two fortnightly city magazines *Tip* and *Zitty* are indispensable sources of day-to-day information about what is happening in Berlin. Editorially, *Zitty* leans towards the alternative Left, with a critical eye and a sensitive finger on the pulse of the times. The programme section not only provides a clear, extensive listing of TV, radio, cinema, theatre, music, readings and what not, but also includes brief descriptions of many of the events. *Tip* is a bit faddier, more life-style-orientated, but its programme section is just as comprehensive. Whenever urgently in need of something – whether it be a service, new furniture, a car, or (human) company – Berliners pick up a copy of *Zweite Hand*, the local classified advertisement paper.

Radio and TV

Radio and TV broadcast around the clock. Those without cable can receive six television stations via antenna: the four public broadcasting companies ARD, ZDF, NDR and the ex-East-German TV station, DFF, as well as the private stations RTL plus and SATURDAY 1. The leading radio company is the publicly funded SFB with four channels: SFB 1 with light music and entertainment; SFB 2, information and pop music; SFB 3, a combination of classical music and culture; and SFB 4, the 'noise-and-chatter-for-kids' music station. The former US-sponsored propaganda station RIAS now has two frequencies: pop and 'post-Cold-War' information (RIAS 2) and culture (RIAS 1)

The DS (Deutschlandsender) Kultur programmes are excellent. The youth radio DT (Deutschland-Treff) Jugendradio produces popular programmes. Among the 'new' stations in the East, Radio Aktuell deserves mentioning:

the Berliner Rundfunk's 'Programme from the Federal German Capital'.

Post and Telecommunication

Post office business hours are: weekdays 8am–6pm and Saturday 8am–12am. Outside these regular hours, the following post offices are open for full service:

Bahnhof Zoologischer Garten (train station), 24-hour counter.

Hauptbahnhof in Friedrichshain (train station), Monday–Friday 7am–9pm, Saturday 8am–1pm.

Flughafen Tegel (airport), daily 6.30am–9pm.

Bahnhof Friedrichstraße (train station), Monday–Friday 7am–9pm, Saturday 8am–1pm.

Postamt (post office) Alexanderplatz, Rathausstraße 5, Monday–Friday 7am–9pm, Saturday 8am–7pm, Sunday 8am–1pm.

Trying to telephone between East and West Berlin still involves considerable difficulties. The lines which were cut in the 1950s are still not up to Western standards. Experts estimate that service will not reach a normal level until the end of 1992. Until then the following dialling codes apply:

From West to East Berlin: 9.
From East to West Berlin: 849.

Whenever calling you must always remember to dial the appropriate codes first, as numbers are always listed without them. Four-digit district numbers refer to East Berlin; two-digit ones stand for West Berlin.

A few of the telephone information services listed in the West Berlin telephone book are:

Programmes:
Major cinemas A–K: 11511;
Major cinemas L–Z: 11512.
Neighbourhood cinemas: 11514 and 11515.
Travellers' weather service: 11600.
Theatre and concert events: 1156.
Cabaret, variety, etc: 11517.

SPORT & LEISURE

In Berlin practically every green area provides an opportunity for sports. The Schloßpark Charlottenburg in front of Belvedere is where badminton and volleyball players meet. At the Grunewaldsee you can hardly see the path around the lake for all the joggers. There is even (downhill!) skiing on the Teufelsberg and – providing there is enough snow – you will see swarms of people out sledding on every elevation remotely resembling a hill. There are tennis courts in all the districts. The most elegant – exclusively available to members and for classy tournaments – is the Tennis-Club Rot-Weiß in the Grunewald district in Wilmersdorf, Gottfried-von-Cramm-Straße 129, Tel: 5090891.

Horse racing and betting fans will undoubtably enjoy a visit to one of the following tracks:

TRABRENNBAHN MARIENDORF
Mariendorfer Damm 212. Tel: 7401-1.

TRABRENNBAHN KARLSHORST
Hermann-Duncker-Straße 129.
Tel: 5090891.

GALOPPRENNBAHN HOPPEGARTEN
Goetheallee 1,
1271 Dahlwitz-Hoppegarten.
Tel: 5596102.

There are outdoor pools with artificially-produced waves, saunas, sunbathing lawns and plenty of other watersports facilities:

Buschkrugallee 64, Tel: 6066060.

SEZ (SPORT & RECREATION CENTRE),
Leninallee 77, Tel: 43283505.

SPORTS CENTRE SACHSENDAMM
Sachsendamm 1, Tel: 7833003.

The greatest bathing pleasure, however, awaits you at the Strandbad Wannsee lakeside facilities, complete with hooded wicker beach chairs, promenade and Baltic Sea sand in Zehlendorf, south of the island: Insel Schwanenwerder, Am Wannseebadweg, Tel: 8035450.

Theatre and Opera

BERLINER ENSEMBLE
Bertold-Brecht-Platz 1. Tel: 2888150.
DEUTSCHE OPER
Bismarckstraße 34–37. Tel: 3410249.
DEUTSCHE STAATSOPER
Unter den Linden 7. Tel: 2082861.
DEUTSCHES THEATER
Schumannstraße 13a. Tel: 2871221.
FREIE VOLKSBÜHNE
Schaperstraße 24. Tel: 8813742.
FRIEDRICHSTADTPALAST
Friedrichstraße 107. Tel: 248950.
HANSA-THEATER 21
Alt-Moabit 48. Tel: 8813742.
HEBBEL-THEATER
Stresemannstraße 29. Tel: 2510144.
KOMISCHE OPER
Behrenstraße 55–57. Tel: 2292603.
KOMÖDIE AM KURFÜRSTENDAMM
Kurfürstendamm 206. Tel: 8827893.
MAXIM-GORKI-THEATER
Am Festungsgraben 2. Tel: 2082783.
METROPOL-THEATER
Friedrichstraße 101–102.
Tel: 2082715.
PHILHARMONIE UND KAMMERMUSIKSAAL,
Matthäikirchstraße 1. Tel: 2614383.
RENAISSANCE-THEATER
Hardenbergstraße 6. Tel: 3124202.
SCHAUBÜHNE AM LENINER PLATZ
Kurfürstendamm 153. Tel: 890023.
SCHAUSPIELHAUS
Platz der Akademie. Tel: 2272122.
SCHILLER-THEATER
Bismarckstraße 110. Tel: 3195236.
SCHLOßPARKTHEATER
Schloßstraße 48. Tel: 3195236.
THEATER DES WESTENS
Kantstraße 12. Tel: 3121022.
THEATERMANUFAKTUR
Hallesches Ufer 32. Tel: 2510941.
VAGANTENBÜHNE
Kantstraße 12a. Tel: 3124529.
VOLKSBÜHNE
Rosa-Luxemburg-Platz. Tel: 2828978.

Cabaret

BKA
Mehringdamm 34. Tel: 2510112.
DIE DISTEL
Friedrichstraße 101. Tel: 2004704.
QUARTIER
(Variety, cabaret and concert.)
Potsdamer Straße 96. Tel: 2629016.
STACHELSCHWEINE
Europa-Center, Entrance, Tauentzienstraße. Tel: 2614795.
WÜHLMÄUSE
Nürnberger Straße 33. Tel: 2137047.

Advance Booking Information

BOX-OFFICE
Nollendorfplatz 7. Tel: 2151951.
CENTRUM
Meinekestraße 25. Tel: 8827611.
KADEWE
Tauentzienstraße 21. Tel: 248036.
SASSE-HENNING
Kurfürstendamm 24. Tel: 8827360.
THEATERKASSE KIOSK AM ZOO
Kantstraße 3. Tel: 8813603.
THEATERKASSE IM PALASTHOTEL
Karl-Liebknecht-Straße 5,
Beginning of Spandauer Straße.
Tel: 2125258/2125902.
WERTHEIM
Kurfürstendamm 231. Tel: 8822500.

Museums in Dahlem

BOTANISCHER GARTEN
(BOTANICAL GARDEN)
Königin-Luise-Straße 6–8,
Winter daily 9am–4pm,
Summer 9am–8pm.

Brücke Museum
Bussardsteig 9,
Wednesday–Monday 11am–5pm.
Works by the 'Brücke' group.

Domäne Dahlem
Königin-Luise-Straße 49,
daily 9am–6pm.
Everyday life on a Brandenburg Marches farm.

Gemäldegalerie
Arnimallee 23,
Tuesday–Sunday 9am–5pm.
13th–18th-century European painting.

Kupferstichkabinett
Arnimallee 23-27,
Tuesday–Sunday 9am–5pm.
Copperplate etching collection.

Museum für Deutsche Volkskunde
Im Winkel 6–8.
Tuesday–Sunday 9am–5pm.
German folk art.

Museum für Indische Kunst
Besuchereingang Lansstraße 8.
Tuesday–Sunday 9am–5pm.
Eastern Indian art.

Museum für Ostasiatische Kunst
Besuchereingang Lansstraße 8.
Tuesday–Sunday 9am–5pm.
Eastern Asian art.

Museum für Völkerkunde
Besuchereingang Lansstraße 8.
Tuesday–Sunday 9am–5pm.
Ethnology.

Museums in Charlottenburg

Ägyptisches Museum
Schloßstraße 70.
Saturday–Thursday 9am–5pm.
Egyptian art.

Antikenmuseum
Schloßstraße 1.
Saturday–Thursday 9am–5pm.
Art of the ancient world.

Bröhan-Museum
Schloßstraße 1a.
Tuesday–Sunday 10am–6pm.
Art Nouveau design, Art Deco; Berlin Secession and industrial design.

Galerie der Romantik
Schloß Charlottenburg.
Tuesday–Sunday 9am–5pm.

Georg-Kolbe-Museum
Sensburger Allee 25. Daily 10am–5pm.
Berlin sculpture of the 20th century.

Museum für Vor- und Frühgeschichte
Schloß Charlottenburg.
Saturday–Thursday 9am–5pm.
Prehistoric and ancient collections..

Museums in Tiergarten

Bauhaus-Archiv
Klingelhöferstraße 14.
Wednesday–Monday 11am–5pm.

Fragen an die Deutsche Geschichte
Reichstagsgebäude.
Tuesday–Sunday 10am–5pm.

Gedenkstätte Deutscher Widerstand
Stauffenbergstraße 13–14.
Daily 9am–6pm.
German resistance memorial.

Kunstgewerbemuseum
Tiergartenstraße 6.
Tuesday–Saturday 9am–5pm,
Sunday 10am–5 pm.
Arts and crafts.

Musikinstrumenten-Museum
Tiergartenstraße 1.
Tuesday–Saturday 9am–5pm,
Sunday 10am–5pm.
Musical instruments.

Neue Nationalgalerie
Potsdamer Straße 50.
Tuesday–Sunday 9am–5pm.
19th- and 20th-century painting and sculpture.

Special Museums in East Berlin

Berliner Arbeiterleben um 1900
Husemannstraße 12,
Prenzlauer Berg.
Tuesday, Thursday, Saturday 11am–6pm, Wednesday 11am–8pm.
Reconstructed worker's flat: Berlin's working-class living conditions around the turn of the century.

Brecht-Haus
Chausseestraße 125.
Tuesday–Friday 10am–noon,
Thursday 5–7pm,
Saturday 9.30–12am, 12.30am–2pm.
The living and working quarters of Bertold Brecht and Helene Weigel.

Friedrichwerdersche Kirche
Werderscher Markt.
Wednesday–Sunday 9am–6pm,
Friday 10am–6pm.
Works by Karl Friedrich Schinkel.

Friseurmuseum
Husemannstraße 8, Prenzlauer Berg.
Monday, Wednesday 10am–noon and 1–5pm.
Odd and interesting tools of the hairdressing trade.

Gründerzeitmuseum
Hultschiner Damm 333,
Mahlsdorf (Hellersdorf).
Guided tours on Sunday at 11am and noon; otherwise only by prior arrangement. A private collector, quite a character himself, has gathered all kinds of household goods from the 'Gründerzeit' era. He has a great love of bizarre and historical objects.

Johannes-R-Becher-Haus
Majakowskiring 34,
Niederschönhausen.
Tuesday 2–6pm, Wednesday/Thursday 9am–12pm, 2–5pm.
Residence of the poet who wrote the former GDR national anthem, also a literature museum.

Handwerksmuseum
In Mühlendamm,
Monday 10am–5pm,
Tuesday/Wednesday 9am–5pm,
Saturday/Sunday 10am–6pm.
13th–19th-century Berlin trades.

Hundemuseum
Alt Blankenburg 33, Weißensee.
Tuesday, Thursday, Saturday 3–6pm,
Sunday 11am–5pm.
A collection for dog lovers.

Hugenottenmuseum
Platz der Akademie,
Französischer Dom, Mitte.
Monday–Friday 10am–5pm.
The history of the Huguenots in France and Prussia.

Märkisches Museum
Am Köllnischen Park 5, Mitte.
Wednesday, Sunday 9am–6pm.
Thursday, Saturday 9am–5pm;
Friday 9am–4pm.
The cultural and intellectual history of Berlin up to the present.

Museum für Deutsche Geschichte
(taken over by the **Deutsches Historisches Museum**)
Unter den Linden 2, Mitte.
Monday–Thursday 9am–7pm,
Saturday and Sunday 10am–5pm.
Documents and objects from the first communities up to today. Within the next two to three years the 'socialist' perspective will still be reflected.

Museum für Naturkunde
Invalidenstraße 43, Mitte.
Tuesday–Sunday 9:30am–5pm.
Zoology, mineralogy and palaeontology.

Otto-Nagel-Haus
Märkisches Ufer 16–18, Mitte.
Sunday–Thursday 10am–6pm,
Wednesday 10am–8pm.
Proletarian revolutionary art from the national gallery.

Pathologisches Museum der Charité
Charitéstraße, Mitte.
Tuesday and Thursday 2–4pm. (Visitors should call first: Tel: 2863147.)
Anatomical exhibits.

Postmuseum
Leipziger-Straße/Ecke Mauerstraße, Mitte.
Tuesday–Saturday 10am–6pm
The postal service's collection.

Robert-Koch-Museum
Klara-Zetkin-Straße 96, Mitte.
Monday–Friday 1–4pm
(by prior arrangement).
The life of Robert Koch.

Special Museums in West Berlin

Anti-Kriegs-Museum
Genter Straße 9, Wedding.
Daily 4–8pm.
Displays on war and peace.

Berliner Post- und Fernmeldemuseum
An der Urania 15, Schöneberg.
Tuesday–Friday 10am–4pm,
Saturday and Sunday 10am–1pm.
Post office and telecommunication museum.

Berlinische Galerie
Stresemannstraße 110 (Gropius Building), Kreuzberg.
Tuesday–Sunday 10am–6pm.
19th- and 20th-century art.

Berlin-Museum
Lindenstraße 14, Kreuzberg.
Tuesday–Sunday 11am–6pm.
General history of Berlin from the 16th century to the present.

Berliner Panoptikum
Kurfürstendamm 227–8,
Wilmersdorf, Kudamm-Eck.
Daily 10am–11pm
Wax museum.

Friedensmuseum
Stresemannstraße 27, Kreuzberg.
Daily 4–8pm.
Exhibits dealing with arms, the concept of the enemy, and the peace movement.

Haus am Checkpoint Charlie
Friedrichstraße 44, Kreuzberg.
Daily 9am–10pm
Photographs, documents and objects documenting the history of the wall.

Heinrich-Zille-Museum
U-Bahn station Nollendorfplatz, Schöneberg.
Wednesday–Monday 11am–7pm.

Käthe-Kollwitz-Museum
Fasanenstraße 24, Kreuzberg.
Wednesday–Monday 11am–6pm.
Germany's renowned woman painter.

Museum für Verkehr und Technik
Trebbiner Straße 9, Kreuzberg.
Tuesday–Friday 9am–6pm,
Saturday and Sunday 10am–6pm.
Transport, technology and the social aspects of technical culture.

Museumsdorf Düppel,
Clauertstraße 11, Zehlendorf.
May–October: Sunday 10am–1pm.
A reconstructed medieval village.

Polizeihistorische Sammlung
Platz der Luftbrücke 6, Tempelhof.
Monday 2–6pm.
Objects relating to the history and work of the police.

Teddy-Museum
Kurfürstendamm-Karree (1st floor), Wilmersdorf.
Wednesday–Monday 3–10pm.

Zucker-Museum
Amrumer Straße 32, Wedding.
(Phone in advance, Tel: 3147520.)
Sugar museum.

Castles and Gardens

Jageschloß Grunewald
Tuesday–Sunday 10am–4pm.

Schloß Glienicke
At Wannsee.
For information regarding guided tours, Tel: 8053041.
The garden is open daily.

Schloß und Landschaftsgarten Pfaueninsel (Peacock Island Castle and Landscape Garden)
Daily winter, 10am–4pm;
summer 8am–8pm.

Schloß Tegel (Humboldt Museum)
Wednesday and Sunday 2–6pm.

Schloß Köpenick
Wednesday–Saturday 9am–5pm,
Sunday 10am–6pm.

Schloß Niederschönhausen
The castle is not open to the public.

Schloß Friedrichsfelde
Guided tours: Tuesday–Friday 3pm;
Saturday and Sunday 11am, 1pm, 3pm.

A

B

C

D

E, F

G, H, J

K

L

M

N, O

P, Q

R

S

T, U, V

W, Z

Art & Photo Credits

Photography	**Christine Engel** *and*
12, 13, 15, 19, 120	**Ullstein**
22	**Ullstein/ADN-Zantralbil**
6, 23	**Ullstein/Gerd Hilde**
16	**Ullstein/Günter Schneider**
21	**Ullstein/Bernd Thiele**
Cover Design	**Klaus Geisler**
Cartography	**Berndtson & Berndtson**

NOTES

NOTES

NOTES

NOTES

Konradshöhe
TEGEL
WITTENAU
NIEDER-
E 26
Tegeler See
TEGEL
Tegelort
REINICKENDORF
PARCELLSUSBAD
SEIDELSTR.
A 111
Bernauer Str
Flughafen Berlin-Tegel
A 11
AFRIKAN. STR.
WEDDING
OSLOERSTR.
SPANDAU
HASELHORST
Schumacher Damm
LEOPOLDPL.
Seestraße
Zitadelle Spandau
Gedenkstätte Plötzensee
WEDD
PAUL-STERN-STR.
J. - KAISER PL.
PULITZSTR.
RATH. SPANDAU
SIEMENSSTADT
Gördeler Damm
SPANDAU
A 10
Spree
Stadtring
TIERGARTEN
TURMSTR.
RUHLEBEN
Schloß Charlottenburg
CHARLOTTENBURG
Reichstag
Siegessäule
Deutsche Oper
Straße des 17.Jun
Heerstraße
Olympiastadion
Brandenbu
Zoologischer Garten
THEOD. HEUSS PL.
BISMARCK STR.
ZOOLOG. GARTEN
2
5
Potsdamer Str.
Havel chaussee
Gedächtniskirche
Messegelände
Funkturm
Kurfürstendamm
Deutschlandhalle
WESTKREUZ
SPEICHERN-STR.
NOLLENDORFPL.
Teufelsberg
Avus
FEHRBELLINER PL.
BAYER PL.
WILMERSDORF
GRUNEWALD
A 10
BERLINER STR.
Rathaus Schöneberg
SCHÖN
BERG
E 51
A 104
SCHÖNEBERG
Grunewaldturm
Schmargendorf
Jagdschloß Grunewald
FRIEDR. WILHELM PL.
A 103
BREITENBACH PL.
Havel
PRIESTERWEG
Krumme Lanke
A 51
DAHLEM
Botanischer Garten
RATH. STEGLITZ
Havelchaussee
THIELPL.
Schlachtensee
Unter den Eichen
STEGLITZ
ZEHLENDORF
Avus
KRUMME LANKE
1
NIKOLASSEE
Potsdamer Chaussee
NIKOLASSEE
Museumsdorf
ZEHLENDORF
LANKWITZ
LICHTERFELDE

Berlin
1600 m / 0,1 miles
BLANKENBURG
Gottwald-Allee
SCHÖNHAUSEN
Klement-
MALCHOW
Schloß-
Niederschönhausen
Wartenberg
PANKOW
HEINERSDORF
109
158
PANKOW
FALKENBERG
WEISSENSEE
PANKOW (VINETASTR.)
PRENZLAUER
Falkenberger Chaussee
HOHENSCHÖNHAUSEN
Straße
Ostseestr.
BORNHOLMER STR.
BERG
Greifswalder Straße 2
VOLTASTR.
DIMITROFFSTR.
MARZAHN
MITTE
Leninallee
LICHTENBERG
Museumsinsel
Fernsehturm
ALEXANDERPL.
Wuhlgarten
FRANKFURTER TOR
Marienkirche
Frankfurter Allee 5/1
Dom
FRIEDRICHS-HAIN
LICHTENBERG
STADTMITTE
★ Former site of Checkpoint Charlie
OSTKREUZ
BIESDORF
Tierpark
HALLESCHES TOR
KOTTBUSER TOR
SCHLES. TOR
FRIEDRICHSFELDE
KREUZBERG
TIERPARK
Puschkin Allee
HERMANNPL.
Karl-Marx-Straße
Sonnen Allee
NEU-KÖLLN
TREPTOW
KARLSHORST
Flughafen Berlin-Tempelhof
LEINESTR.
Trabrennbahn
NEUKÖLLN
Schnellerstraße
A 102
A 10
GRENZALLEE
OBERSCHÖNE-WEIDE
TEMPEL-HOF
NIEDER-SCHÖNEWEIDE
BRITZ
Teltow-Kanal
Buschkrugallee
ADLERSHOF
Alder Gestell
MARIENDORF
JOHANNISTHAL
96
ALT MARIENDORF
BRITZ - SÜD
179
Erholungspark (BUGA)
BUCKOW